REFLECT

LISTENING & SPEAKING

JONATHAN BYGRAVE

NATIONAL
GEOGRAPHIC
LEARNING

Australia · Brazil · Mexico · Singapore · United Kingdom · United States

National Geographic Learning,
a Cengage Company

Reflect 5 Listening & Speaking
Author: Jonathan Bygrave

Publisher: Sherrise Roehr
Executive Editor: Laura Le Dréan
Senior Development Editor: Andrew Gitzy
Director of Global Marketing: Ian Martin
Product Marketing Manager: Tracy Baillie
Senior Content Project Manager: Mark Rzeszutek
Media Researcher: Stephanie Eenigenburg
Art Director: Brenda Carmichael
Senior Designer: Lisa Trager
Operations Coordinator: Hayley Chwazik-Gee
Manufacturing Buyer: Mary Beth Hennebury
Composition: MPS Limited

Student Book ISBN: 978-0-357-44915-8
Student Book with Online Practice: 978-0-357-44921-9

National Geographic Learning
200 Pier 4 Boulevard
Boston, MA 02210

Locate your local office at **international.cengage.com/region**

Visit National Geographic Learning online at **ELTNGL.com**
Visit our corporate website at **www.cengage.com**

Printed in Mexico
Print Number: 01   Print Year: 2021

SCOPE AND SEQUENCE

SPEAKING & PRONUNCIATION	GRAMMAR	CRITICAL THINKING	REFLECT ACTIVITIES
Build interest in a story Thought groups	Past forms for storytelling	Speculate and predict	▶ Imagine your life as a story ▶ Analyze a narrative ▶ Outline a story ▶ **UNIT TASK** Tell a story with a moral
Acknowledge other arguments Intonation in questions and statements	Noun clauses	Use current trends to imagine the future	▶ Rank the pros and cons of fast fashion ▶ Estimate the impact of fashion trends ▶ Brainstorm solutions to issues in fast fashion ▶ **UNIT TASK** Make a plan to save a fashion company
Refer to and describe visuals Word stress	Reduced adjective clauses	Evaluate sources of information	▶ Consider how ideas about cleanliness change over time ▶ Evaluate sources of information from the past and present ▶ Explain how advertising has influenced hygiene and health ▶ **UNIT TASK** Compare ads for products from different times in history
Describe trends in graphs and charts Expressing emotions	Passive voice with modals	Extend ideas	▶ Consider how animals lead ▶ Extend learning to new topics ▶ Evaluate leadership styles ▶ **UNIT TASK** Give leadership advice

SPEAKING & PRONUNCIATION	GRAMMAR	CRITICAL THINKING	REFLECT ACTIVITIES
Introduce contrasting information Focus words in contrasting information	Comparative forms	Avoid stereotypes	▶ Analyze what makes you laugh ▶ Consider the role of humor in your life ▶ Tell a joke ▶ **UNIT TASK** Give a presentation about humor in your country
Present persuasively Linking words	Reporting verbs	Identify criteria and constraints	▶ Evaluate the pros and cons of living environments ▶ Propose a solution to an urban problem ▶ Consider initiatives for improving urban sustainability ▶ **UNIT TASK** Present a plan for a new public space
Give an overview of a presentation Intonation in short exchanges	Future forms	Consider an issue from various perspectives	▶ Assess the impact of tourism ▶ Consider tourism from various perspectives ▶ Reflect on tourism preferences ▶ **UNIT TASK** Present a plan for an online tourist experience
Summarize a lecture Thought groups and intonation	Gerunds/ infinitives as subjects; preposition + gerund	Relate concepts to your experience	▶ Consider how data can help a sports team ▶ Discuss how data can improve your life ▶ Examine how you respond to pressure ▶ **UNIT TASK** Summarize a presentation on athletic performance

CONNECT TO IDEAS

Reflect Listening & Speaking features relevant, global content to engage students while helping them acquire the academic language and skills they need. Specially-designed activities give students the opportunity to reflect on and connect ideas and language to their academic, work, and personal lives.

National Geographic photography and content invite students to investigate the world and discuss high-interest topics.

Watch & Speak and **Listen & Speak** sections center on high-interest video and audio that students will want to talk about as they build academic listening and speaking skills.

CONNECT TO ACADEMIC SKILLS

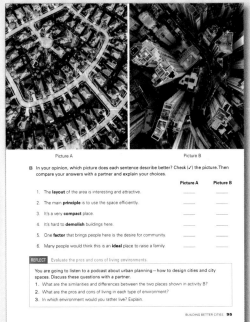

Scaffolded activities build confidence and provide students with a clear path to achieving final outcomes.

Qhouurunnisa' Endang Wahyudi performs a football trick in Shah Alam, Selangor, Malaysia.

> **SPEAKING SKILL** Summarize a lecture
> Follow these steps when you summarize a lecture or presentation.
>
> | | |
> |---|---|
> | **State the topic** | *The topic of the presentation is . . .* |
> | **Define the topic** | *It refers to . . .*
 It involves . . . |
> | **Give key information** | *It is important to note that . . .*
 The speaker emphasizes that . . . |
> | **Give examples** | *The first/second example that the speaker gives is . . .*
 Here, . . . / In this example, . . . |

H APPLY Listen again to the student summarizing the lecture. Complete the summary with the words that she uses.

The topic of the presentation is visualization. Visualization
¹ _____ a technique that can help athletes improve their
performance. It ² _____ imagining that they are performing an
action in their minds. They think about doing the action.

142 UNIT 8

Reflect activities give students the opportunity to think critically about what they are learning and check their understanding.

Focused academic **listening** and **speaking skills** help students communicate with confidence.

Picture A   Picture B

B In your opinion, which picture does each sentence describe better? Check (✓) the picture. Then compare your answers with a partner and explain your choices.

	Picture A	Picture B
1. The **layout** of the area is interesting and attractive.	___	___
2. The main **principle** is to use the space efficiently.	___	___
3. It's a very **compact** place.	___	___
4. It's hard to **demolish** buildings here.	___	___
5. One **factor** that brings people here is the desire for community.	___	___
6. Many people would think this is an **ideal** place to raise a family.	___	___

REFLECT Evaluate the pros and cons of living environments.

You are going to listen to a podcast about urban planning—how to design cities and city spaces. Discuss these questions with a partner.
1. What are the similarities and differences between the two places shown in activity B?
2. What are the pros and cons of living in each type of environment?
3. In which environment would you rather live? Explain.

BUILDING BETTER CITIES **95**

UNIT TASK Compare ads from different times in history.

You are going to give a presentation about the differences between two ads for a product, one from the past and one from the present. You will explain what each shows about society at the time it was created. Use the ideas, vocabulary, and skills from the unit.

I MODEL Listen to a student describing two ads. Take notes in the chart. Then compare your notes with a partner.

	Old magazine ad	Current social media ad	Reason for differences
The first thing you notice			
The images			
The text			
The advertisers			

THE HISTORY OF HYGIENE **51**

GRAMMAR Reduced adjective clauses
Remember: An adjective clause is a dependent clause that gives more information about a noun. Subject adjective clauses begin with a relative pronoun, such as *who, which, that,* or *whose.* A verb follows the relative pronoun.

> Take a look at the <u>text</u> *that describes the benefits of using the soap.*

We can reduce or shorten some subject adjective clauses. To do this, take out the relative pronoun, the verb *be* (if the clause has one), and use the *-ing* form of the main verb.

> Take a look at the text ~~that describes~~ *describing the benefits of using the soap.*
> The number of people ~~who used~~ *using public baths* increased.
> He was looking for the document ~~that was~~ *sitting on the printer.*

If the verb is in the passive voice, take out the relative pronoun and the verb *be.*

> Photos ~~that are~~ *shared digitally* cost nothing.

K GRAMMAR Underline the adjective clause in each sentence. Then check (✓) the four sentences where the adjective clause can be reduced.
1. ___ The man who is cleaning the dishes in the ad looks very unhappy.
2. ___ The sofa that the family is sitting on is very old-fashioned.
3. ___ Social media stars who are followed by a lot of people are often paid to post about a product.
4. ___ The bottle that she is holding contains an expensive perfume.
5. ___ Advertisers used to make many wild promises that consumers believed.
6. ___ All magazines now rely on the money that is earned from advertising.
7. ___ Almost half the people who saw the online advertisement clicked on it.
8. ___ The ads are aimed at children whose parents want to buy them a present.

L GRAMMAR Rewrite the four sentences that you checked (✓) in activity K with reduced adjective clauses.
1. _____
2. _____
3. _____
4. _____

THE HISTORY OF HYGIENE **53**

Clear models, relevant grammar, and step-by-step planning give students the support they need to complete the final speaking task successfully.

CONNECT TO ACHIEVEMENT

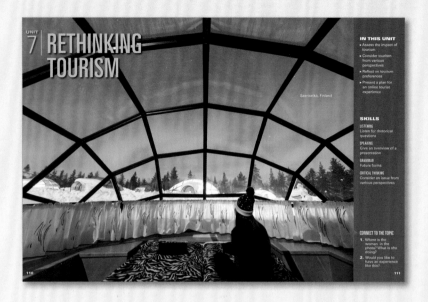

Reflect at the end of the unit is an opportunity for formative assessment. Students review the skills and vocabulary they have gained.

DIGITAL RESOURCES

TEACH lively, engaging lessons that get students to participate actively. The Classroom Presentation Tool helps teachers to present the Student's Book pages, play audio and video, and increase participation by providing a central focus for the class.

LEARN AND TRACK with Online Practice and Student's eBook. For students, the mobile-friendly platform reinforces learning through additional and adaptive practice. For instructors, progress-tracking is made easy through the shared gradebook.

ASSESS learner performance and progress with the ExamView® Assessment Suite. For assessment, teachers create and customize tests and quizzes easily using the ExamView® Assessment Suite, available online.

ACKNOWLEDGMENTS

The Authors and Publisher would like to acknowledge the teachers around the world who participated in the development of *Reflect*.

A special thanks to our Advisory Board for their valuable input during the development of this series.

ADVISORY BOARD

Dr. Mansoor S. Almalki, Taif University, Saudi Arabia; **John Duplice**, Sophia University, Japan; **Heba Elhadary**, Gulf University for Science and Technology, Kuwait; **Hind Elyas**, Niagara College, Saudi Arabia; **Cheryl House**, ILSC Education Group, Canada; **Xiao Luo**, BFUS International, China; **Daniel L. Paller,** Kinjo Gakuin University, Japan; **Ray Purdy**, ELS Education Services, USA; **Sarah Symes,** Cambridge Street Upper School, USA.

GLOBAL REVIEWERS

ASIA

Michael Crawford, Dokkyo University, Japan; **Ronnie Hill**, RMIT University Vietnam, Vietnam; **Aaron Nurse**, Golden Path Academics, Vietnam; **Simon Park**, Zushi Kaisei, Japan; **Aunchana Punnarungsee**, Majeo University, Thailand.

LATIN AMERICA AND THE CARIBBEAN

Leandro Aguiar, inFlux, Brazil; **Sonia Albertazzi-Osorio**, Costa Rica Institute of Technology, Costa Rica; **Auricea Bacelar**, Top Seven Idiomas, Brazil; **Natalia Benavides**, Universidad de Los Andes, Colombia; **James Bonilla**, Global Language Training UK, Colombia; **Diego Bruekers Deschamp**, Inglês Express, Brazil; **Josiane da Rosa**, Hello Idiomas, Brazil; **Marcos de Campos Bueno**, It's Cool International, Brazil; **Sophia De Carvalho**, Ingles Express, Brazil; **André Luiz dos Santos**, IFG, Brazil; **Oscar Gomez-Delgado**, Universidad de los Andes, Colombia; **Ruth Elizabeth Hibas**, Inglês Express, Brazil; **Rebecca Ashley Hibas**, Inglês Express, Brazil; **Cecibel Juliao**, UDELAS University, Panama; **Rosa Awilda López Fernández**, School of Languages UNAPEC University, Dominican Republic; **Isabella Magalhães**, Fluent English Pouso Alegre, Brazil; **Gabrielle Marchetti**, Teacher's House, Brazil; **Sabine Mary**, INTEC, Dominican Republic; **Miryam Morron**, Corporación Universitaria Americana, Colombia; **Mary Ruth Popov**, Ingles Express, Ltda., Brazil; **Leticia Rodrigues Resende**, Brazil; **Margaret Simons**, English Center, Brazil.

MIDDLE EAST

Abubaker Alhitty, University of Bahrain, Bahrain; **Jawaria Iqbal**, Saudi Arabia; **Rana Khan**, Algonquin College, Kuwait; **Mick King**, Community College of Qatar, Qatar; **Seema Jaisimha Terry**, German University of Technology, Oman.

USA AND CANADA

Thomas Becskehazy, Arizona State University, AZ; **Robert Bushong**, University of Delaware, DE; **Ashley Fifer**, Nassau Community College, NY; **Sarah Arva Grosik**, University of Pennsylvania, PA; **Carolyn Ho**, Lone Star College-CyFair, TX; **Zachary Johnsrud**, Norquest College, Canada; **Caitlin King**, IUPUI, IN; **Andrea Murau Haraway**, Global Launch / Arizona State University, AZ; **Bobbi Plante**, Manitoba Institute of Trades and Technology, Canada; **Michael Schwartz**, St. Cloud State University, MN; **Pamela Smart-Smith**, Virginia Tech, VA; **Kelly Smith**, English Language Institute, UCSD Extension, CA; **Karen Vallejo**, University of California, CA.

THE ART OF STORYTELLING

Rappers take turns
performing in Union Square
Park in New York City, USA.

CONNECT TO THE TOPIC

1. What is happening in the photo? Do you think this is a kind of storytelling?

2. Is there a story that has had a powerful effect on you? What was the story? What was the effect?

PREPARE TO LISTEN

A VOCABULARY Listen to the words. Then read the definitions. Complete the sentences with the correct form of the words. 🔊1.1

---

climax (n) the most exciting moment
conflict (n) a serious disagreement between people or groups
crisis (n) a time of great difficulty or danger
dilemma (n) a situation where you have to make a difficult choice
flaw (n) a fault or weakness, particularly in someone's character
incident (n) an event, often unusual
moral (n) a message about life that you get from a story
obstacle (n) something that stops you from going somewhere or getting something
overcome (v) to defeat a person or thing
status (n) a person's position of respect in a group

---

1. In action-adventure movies, the hero usually has to _____ the bad guy and stop something terrible from happening.

2. I don't like movies where nothing happens. If there are no exciting events or unexpected _____, it's just boring.

3. Romantic comedies are always the same. Two characters are in love, but there are a lot of _____ that stop them from being together.

4. I love thrillers. The excitement builds slowly, and at the _____ you find out who the killer is.

5. Sometimes in movies or TV series, the main characters have a lot of _____ that make them seem weak at first, but we still want them to succeed.

6. At the beginning of some movies, the main character is a child. As the movie goes on, they get older, they gain more power and more _____, but they also become less happy.

7. In James Bond movies, there is always a _____ between James Bond and a bad guy who wants to rule the world. The ending is usually a fight between them.

8. Children's stories usually have a _____ or lesson, for example, *don't give up*, *be honest*, or *be a good friend*.

9. I saw a science fiction film about our world in the future. There was a _____ because the sun was dying. It's hard to imagine a bigger problem!

10. In superhero movies, the heroes often face a _____. They have to choose between living a normal life and having fun or using their powers to help other people.

B PERSONALIZE Discuss the questions with a partner.

1. How do you deal with **conflict**?
2. Think of a specific problem you have had. How did you **overcome** it?
3. Is social **status** important to you? Explain.

C Listen to two students discussing a film. Choose the correct answers. 🎧1.2

1. What discovery does the woman make?
   a. That she's a scientist   b. A way to gain more status   c. A way to stop getting old
2. What is her biggest flaw in the film?
   a. She doesn't like conflict.   b. She's always late.   c. She's loves being famous.
3. What obstacles does she have to overcome?
   a. No one thinks she can succeed.   b. No one likes her.   c. People think she is too serious.
4. Who does she have a conflict with?
   a. Her family   b. The moral of the film   c. Another scientist
5. What is the moral of the film?
   a. Don't stop trying.   b. Give up now.   c. Love is stronger than hate.

REFLECT Imagine your life as a story.

You're going to listen to a lecture about how to structure a story. First, imagine that you're famous, and a film director wants to tell your life story. Complete the chart. Then ask and answer the questions with a partner.

1. Why did you become famous?	
2. What is your biggest flaw?	
3. What is the biggest obstacle that you have to overcome?	
4. Who do you have a conflict with?	
5. What is the moral of the story?	

HOW TO STRUCTURE A GOOD STORY

The balcony scene
from *Romeo and Juliet*

A PREVIEW Look at the photo.
What do you know about the story,
Romeo and Juliet? Do you think it's
a good story?

B MAIN IDEAS Listen to the lecture. Complete the infographic with the correct words. 🎧 1.3

changed	climax	crisis	incident	interesting	obstacles

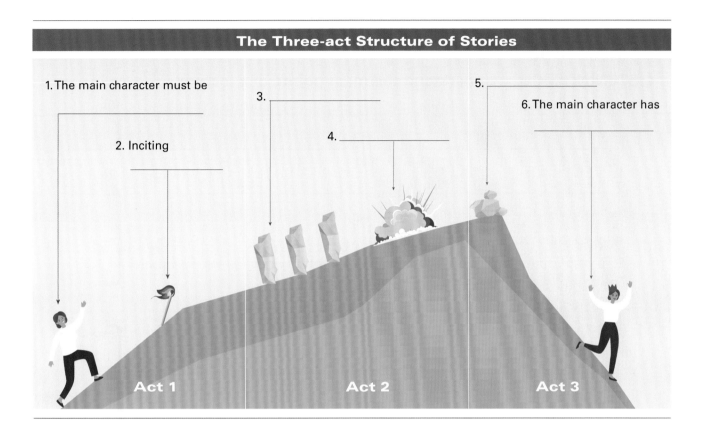

The Three-act Structure of Stories

1. The main character must be _____

2. Inciting _____

3. _____

4. _____

5. _____

6. The main character has _____

Act 1   Act 2   Act 3

C DETAILS Listen again. Choose the correct answer. 🎧 1.3

1. What do audiences like to see in main characters?
   a. People who are nice
   b. People who are likeable
   c. People who have flaws

2. What is the result of the inciting incident on the main character?
   a. They have a new goal.
   b. They fall in love.
   c. They make a mistake.

3. Where do the internal obstacles come from?
   a. The main character's mind
   b. Other people in the story
   c. A conflict or dilemma

4. What must Romeo and Juliet choose between?
   a. Friends and enemies
   b. Love and family
   c. Marrying and not marrying

5. What does the crisis at the end of act 2 force the main character to do?
   a. To lose control
   b. To find out what is wrong
   c. To change and grow

6. When does a story NOT end happily?
   a. When the main character changes
   b. When the main character doesn't change
   c. When the main character acts quickly

D PHRASES TO KNOW Work with a partner. Discuss the meaning of these phrases from the lecture. Then take turns answering the questions.

1. What has been the biggest **turning point** in your life so far?

2. What has been the **low point** of your week so far?

LISTENING SKILL   Understand the main points of a lecture

There are several ways to identify the main or most important points a speaker is making.

1. Listen for signposts.

The key is . . .	*What's essential is . . .*	*Basically,*	*Ultimately,*
The point is . . .	*What matters is . . .*	*Essentially,*	

   Basically, *in act 3 the main character has to show that they have changed.*

2. Listen for repetition.

   Act 2 also usually has **a crisis** *where everything goes wrong for the main character.* **The crisis***, then, is the lowest point for the main character.*

3. Listen for examples.

   In story terms, people who are nice are not very interesting. Think about **Gru in** **Despicable Me** *or* **Rey in** **Star Wars***.*

E APPLY Listen. Complete the extracts from the lecture with a signpost. 🎧 **1.4**

1. Act 1 sets up the world of the story and the main character's place in that world. _____ our interest in the main character.

2. Audiences are interested in people who have flaws and weaknesses. _____ that in act 1 the audience needs to be interested in the main character and what happens to them.

3. For example, the main character might fall in love, or discover a secret, or do something wrong and lose status. _____ that the inciting incident gives the main character a new goal.

4. The main character wants something, but there are a lot of obstacles in their way, and they have to overcome these obstacles. _____, the conflict is between the main character and the obstacles.

5. This crisis is usually at the end of act 2, and it's the low point for the main character. _____, it's the moment when the main character has to change and grow.

6. Act 3 contains the climax of the story. And in this part, _____ that the main character shows that they have changed and learned and grown.

F APPLY Listen to the speakers talk about these topics. What main point does the speaker emphasize? What method does the speaker use to signal an important point? ▶ 1.5

Topic	Main point emphasized	Method		
		Repetition	Example	Signpost
1. Video streaming services				
2. Shakespeare				
3. Successful movies				

REFLECT Analyze a narrative.

Work with a partner. Think of a film or play you have both seen or a story you have both read. Discuss the details of the story and complete the chart.

Act 1	Main character	
	Situation	
	Inciting incident	
Act 2	New goal	
	Obstacles	
	Crisis	
Act 3	Climax	
	Change in main character	
	Moral of the story	

Dance can be a form of storytelling. Chinese Shaolin monks perform the ballet, "Sutra."

PREPARE TO WATCH

A VOCABULARY Listen to the words in bold. Then read three true stories about wild animals. Write each word next to its definition. 🎧 1.6

a. I was sightseeing in a small boat in New Zealand when I found myself right next to a whale and her calf. I turned to look for my camera, **tripped over** my bag, and fell down! Right then, the mother whale jumped out of the water. Her **entire** body left the water, and she landed with a huge splash. I worried that if she jumped again, she might land on the boat and **crush** it. Fortunately, she didn't. Unfortunately, I didn't get a photo.

b. Years ago, I found a kookaburra, which is a bird here in Australia, in my backyard. He was clearly tired and suffering from **exhaustion**. I made him a tall wooden **platform** and put him there, in a box. After a few days, he came and sat on my shoulder when I was outside. After a week, he came very close to my face, almost **leaning** on it. Then, after two weeks, he suddenly flew away. But about a year later, a big kookaburra flew down and landed on my shoulder. He sat there for a while and then flew away. It was incredible!

c. Last summer, I was hiking in the mountains when I came across a black bear. He was **sniffing** some garbage, looking for food. I was terrified. I thought, "I need a **weapon**," but all I had was a small knife, and you can't **stab** a big black bear with a three-inch knife. Then from behind me came a teenage girl. She picked up a rock, threw it at the bear, shouted at him, and **roared** like a lion. The bear ran off. That girl was my hero!

1. _____ (v) taking in air loudly through your nose to smell something

2. _____ (n) a state of great tiredness

3. _____ (n) something that can hurt or kill other people

4. _____ (adj) whole; all of something

5. _____ (n) a flat surface that is raised above the ground

6. _____ (v) fell or nearly fell because your foot hit something

7. _____ (v) put a knife into something in order to hurt or kill it

8. _____ (v) resting on or against something

9. _____ (v) press something very hard so that it is broken, made flat, or destroyed

10. _____ (v) made a loud, angry noise like a lion

B PERSONALIZE Discuss these questions with a partner.

1. Which of the three true stories in activity A do you find the most interesting? Explain.

2. Which animal would you most like to see in the wild? Explain.

3. Have you had any interesting experiences with wild animals? If so, what happened?

C Take the Wild Animals Quiz. Explain your answers to a partner.

WILD ANIMALS

What should you do if you meet these animals in the wild?

1. Crocodiles and alligators
   a. run away
   b. stay completely still
   c. play dead

2. Sharks
   a. stay where you are
   b. swim away calmly
   c. swim away fast

3. Snakes
   a. just ignore them
   b. try to scare them away
   c. walk away slowly

4. Cougars
   a. stay completely still
   b. look away and run
   c. look it in the eye and back away slowly

5. Wolves
   a. don't make eye contact, and try to hide
   b. make eye contact and back away slowly
   c. roar like a lion

REFLECT Outline a story.

Before you watch a video about one explorer's adventure, outline your own story in the wild.

Imagine you are sleeping alone in a tent at night. Suddenly, you hear a lion sniffing around your tent. Decide what happens next and how the story ends. Tell a partner your story.

A NIGHT ALONE WITH LIONS

A young lioness on a night hunt in South Africa

CRITICAL THINKING   Speculate and predict

Before you listen to a story, lecture, or other information, it can be helpful to predict what you think you will hear. You can use the information that is available or simply speculate or make guesses. This helps you to engage with the topic and makes comprehension easier. Then, while you listen, compare your predictions with what you actually hear.

A APPLY You are going to watch a video of Dr. Amy Dickman, a National Geographic Explorer. Read the title and look at the photograph. Speculate and predict what will happen. Share your ideas with a partner.

COMMUNICATION TIP

When Amy Dickman tells her story, she uses the simple present to talk about events in the past. We often do this to make a story more dramatic and exciting.

B MAIN IDEAS Watch the video. Read the statements. Write T for *True* or F for *False*. Then correct the three false statements. ▶ 1.1

1. _____ Dr. Dickman felt nervous because it was her first time sleeping in the bush in Tanzania.

2. _____ She had to sleep in a tent on a platform above the ground.

3. _____ During the night, a lion appeared.

4. _____ When Dickman heard a lion, she looked for things to defend herself.

5. _____ She found a big knife and deodorant spray in her bag.

6. _____ The lion fell asleep on the tent, and Dickman got very hot.

7. _____ Dickman fell asleep while the lion was sleeping.

8. _____ She woke up in the morning and realized it was a dream.

C MAIN IDEAS Work with a partner. Complete the chart with the events from activity B (1–8). Then write the moral of the story with your own ideas.

Act 1	Events	
	Inciting incident	
Act 2	Events	
	Crisis	
Act 3	Events	
	Climax	
	Moral of the story:	

D DETAILS Choose the correct answers. Then watch the video again and check. ▶ 1.1

1. Amy Dickman _____ there were a lot of lions in the area.

   a. knew that   b. didn't know that   c. hoped that

2. Dickman _____ in a tent on the ground.

   a. was hoping to sleep   b. was expecting to sleep   c. was used to sleeping

3. When she first lay down in the tent, she tried not to be _____.

   a. too brave   b. too scared   c. too sensible

4. The lion was _____ her tent.

   a. interested in   b. scared of   c. angry about

5. She knew that the knife and the deodorant _____ protect her from the lion.

   a. might   b. would   c. wouldn't

6. When the lion fell asleep, Dickman was _____.

   a. surprised   b. relieved   c. confused

LEARNING TIP

When telling a story, speakers may use one of these phrases to introduce what they are thinking. When you hear one of these phrases, a speaker is probably sharing thoughts or reactions.

And I was like . . .   *And I think . . .*   *And I thought . . .*

E Listen and complete the excerpts with a phrase from the video. 🎧 1.7

1. They were up on these big platforms. _____, "Oh, that's so much better than I thought."

2. And a guy comes out and he says, "Oh, did you miss your tent?" _____, "Oh, that *is* my tent!"

3. The tent's gone back to its normal shape. _____, "Did I dream that?"

Tell a story with a moral.

You are going to tell a story with a moral. Your story can be something that happened to you, to a friend, or to someone in your family. You will use the three-act structure to tell your story. Use the ideas, vocabulary, and skills from the unit.

F MODEL Listen to a student tell a story. Complete the chart. 🎧 1.8

Act 1	1. Main character	
	2. Situation	
	3. Inciting incident	
Act 2	4. New goal	
	5. Obstacles	
	6. Crisis	
Act 3	7. Climax	
	8. Moral of story	

G DISCUSS What other morals do you often find in stories? Make a list with your partner. Which ones do you find particularly important or true?

It's important to be optimistic.   *Be careful who you trust.*

Taxi driver, Russia, 1965

H NOTICE THE GRAMMAR Complete the sentence from the story with past forms. With a partner, discuss why you chose each verb form.

He [1]_____ (get back) in his taxi even though he

[2]_____ (drive) all day, and he

[3]_____ (go back) to the hotel where he

[4]_____ (drop off) his last passenger.

GRAMMAR   Past forms for storytelling

Use the **simple past** to talk about a completed action in the past.

*When my grandparents first **got** married, they **lived** in a one-room apartment.*

Use the **past continuous** to talk about an action in progress in the past.

*At the time, my grandfather **was working** as a taxi driver.*

The **simple past** often interrupts the **past continuous**.

*He **was finishing** work one day when he **found** some money in the taxi.*

Use the **past perfect** to show that one past event happened before another.

*He went back to the hotel where **he had dropped off** his last passenger.*
       2nd   1st

Use the **past perfect continuous** to show that an event was in progress for a period of time before another event in the past.

*He went back to the hotel even though he **had been driving** all day.*
       2nd   1st

I GRAMMAR Complete the sentences with the correct past form of the verb.

a. While we [1]_____ (have) dinner, I heard a big noise in the

garden. I [2]_____ (run) outside and [3]_____

(see) a fox jump over the fence. Unfortunately, the fox [4]_____

(take) one of the chickens.

b. It was late evening, and I was tired. I [5]_____ (hike)

through the mountains all day. As the sun [6]_____ (set),

I suddenly [7]_____ (hear) a sound and [8]_____

(see) a cougar. I realized that it [9]_____ (follow) me for

a while.

c. Last weekend, I [10]_____ (work) outside in the garden when

I heard a voice. I [11]_____ (look) around, but I couldn't see

anyone. Then I [12]_____ (hear) it again but still, there was no

one. Finally, I [13]_____ (see) my neighbor's pet bird in the tree.

It [14]_____ (escape). It was a cockatoo, and they can talk.

PRONUNCIATION   Thought groups 🔊 1.9

When speaking, we tend to divide language into phrases called thought groups. These are groups of words that express one idea or thought. Using correct thought groups will make you sound more natural and fluent. Thought groups are separated from each other by intonation and slight pauses.

I believe that honesty / is always the best policy / and my grandfather was a great example of this.

A thought group must be meaningful, such as words in a clause or phrase.

J   PRONUNCIATION Listen and notice the thought groups. Listen again and repeat. 🔊 1.10

1. One evening / my grandfather arrived home / and found some money / in the back seat of his taxi.

2. It wasn't a lot of money / but for my grandparents / any amount of money / seemed like a lot.

3. He got back in his taxi / even though he had been driving all day / and he went back to the hotel / where he had dropped off his last passenger.

K   PRONUNCIATION Practice saying this excerpt with a partner. Mark the logical thought groups with a slash (/). You can make different choices depending on what you want to emphasize. Then listen and compare. 🔊 1.11

Eventually, the man showed up. He'd been having dinner, and he didn't even realize he'd lost the money. When my grandfather saw the man, he walked up to him, handed him the money, and said, "Here, I think this belongs to you." Apparently, the man was so surprised that he couldn't speak.

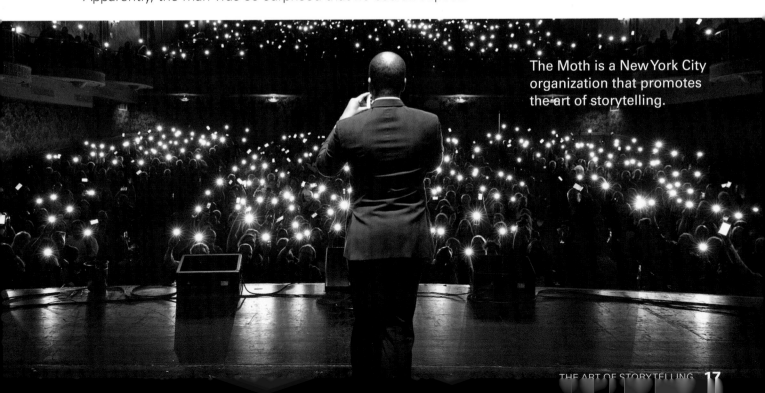

The Moth is a New York City organization that promotes the art of storytelling.

L PLAN Use the chart to outline your story.

The main character(s)	
Act 1 (time, place, background, inciting incident)	
Act 2 (goal, obstacles, crisis)	
Act 3 (climax, change in main character, ending)	
The moral of the story	

SPEAKING SKILL   Build interest in a story

When you tell a story, you want to make it as interesting and enjoyable as possible. There are several ways to do this.

1. Grab the audience's attention at the start. Tell your audience why this story is worth listening to.

   I wasn't there, of course, but this is the story my grandmother used to tell me, and I've never forgotten it.

2. Describe emotions and feelings as well as events. Describe what the main characters were thinking and feeling. You can also describe how you would have felt in that situation.

   He knew exactly what to do. In his situation, I would have given up and gone home.

3. Slow down or use dramatic pauses. This makes the story more exciting.

M APPLY Using your chart in activity L, practice telling your story with a partner. Be sure to build interest in your story. Think about:

▸ your opening sentence. How can you grab your listener's attention?
▸ the inciting incident, crisis, and climax. How can you add feelings and emotions?
▸ good places to slow down and pause. How can that make the story more exciting?

N UNIT TASK Work in groups of three or four. Tell your story and explain the moral. As you listen to your classmates, take notes. How did your classmates build interest in the story?

REFLECT

A Check (✓) the Reflect activities you can do and the academic skills you can use.

☐ imagine your life as a story

☐ analyze a narrative

☐ outline a story

☐ tell a story with a moral

☐ understand the main points of a lecture

☐ build interest in a story

☐ past forms for storytelling

☐ speculate and predict

B Write the vocabulary words from the unit in the correct column. Add any other words that you learned. Circle words you still need to practice.

NOUN	VERB	ADJECTIVE	ADVERB & OTHER

C Reflect on the ideas in the unit as you answer these questions.

1. Which story in this unit did you find most powerful?

_____

_____

2. What is the most important thing you have learned about storytelling?

_____

_____

3. What ideas or skills in this unit will be most useful to you in the future?

_____

_____

UNIT
2 | THE HIGH PRICE
OF FAST FASHION

Models at a fashion show, Milan, Italy

CONNECT TO THE TOPIC

1. Look at the photo. What do you think of the clothes the models are wearing?

2. What do you think the title of the unit means?

PREPARE TO LISTEN

A VOCABULARY Listen to the words in bold. Then read the sentences. Write the correct word next to its definition. 🎧21

▶ The trend of buying more clothes is **accelerating**. People now buy more clothes than in the past. Why do you think this is?

▶ When it comes to shoes, do you have a favorite **brand**? If so, what is it and why is it your favorite?

▶ In order to turn materials such as cotton into clothes, the fashion industry uses around 8,000 different **chemicals**, many of which are dangerous. What do you think the chemicals do?

▶ What is your favorite item of **clothing**? When do you wear it, and why do you like it?

▶ The environmental **cost** of the fashion industry is very high. For example, cotton used to make clothes requires a lot of water. In what other ways might the costs be high?

▶ The **destruction** of unsold clothes leads to a lot of pollution. Why do you think this happens?

▶ The fashion industry is responsible for 10 percent of all carbon **emissions** around the world. That's more than the airline industry. What do you think causes this?

▶ Synthetic **fabrics** are human-made, and natural fabrics are made by nature. Can you name one synthetic fabric and one natural one?

▶ A **gallon** is approximately 3.8 liters. How many gallons of water do you think are needed to grow the cotton for a single t-shirt?

▶ They **manufacture** clothes in many different countries around the world. When you buy clothes, do you care where they were made?

1. _____ (n) materials for making clothes

2. _____ (v) to make in a factory

3. _____ (n) the name a company gives to one product or range of products

4. _____ (v) getting faster

5. _____ (n) solid, liquid, or gas substance or material

6. _____ (n) the act of damaging something so badly that it cannot be fixed

7. _____ (n) a measurement of liquid; 3.8 liters

8. _____ (n) something that goes into the air and harms the environment (e.g., gas)

9. _____ (n) the name for the things we wear

10. _____ (n) what you lose in trying to do something; the price

B PERSONALIZE Work with a partner. Choose four or five questions from activity A and discuss them.

C Listen to two students discussing fast fashion. What do they think are the biggest advantages and disadvantages of fast fashion? Discuss your answers with the class. Do you agree? 🎧 2.2

COMMUNICATION TIP

It is usually not polite to interrupt someone before they have finished speaking. However, there are ways to interrupt and to respond politely.

To interrupt: *Sorry, could I just say/add something? Can I just make a point here?*

To respond: *Sure. Go ahead. Sure, but just let me finish this one point first. What were you going to say?*

D Listen again. Check (✓) the phrases that the speakers use. 🎧 2.2

1. _____ Sorry, could I just say something?

2. _____ Can I just make a point here?

3. _____ Sure. Go ahead.

4. _____ Sure, but just let me finish this one point first.

5. _____ What were you going to say?

REFLECT　　Rank the pros and cons of fast fashion.

Before you listen to a panel discussion on fast fashion, think about these quotations. Then complete the tasks.

"My grandmother has only one shirt in her wardrobe. My mother has three. My daughter's generation [has] 50. And 48 percent of them, she never wears."

—Jack Ma, Founder of Alibaba Group

"Fast fashion isn't free. Someone, somewhere is paying."

—Lucy Siegle, journalist

1. Complete the chart. Make a list of all the pros and cons of fast fashion you can think of.

2. Work with a partner and compare your lists.

3. Decide on the top three pros and cons.

Pros	Cons

THE FACTS ABOUT FAST FASHION

A dress made from clothing that
was thrown away, Prato, Italy

A PHRASES TO KNOW
Work with a partner. Discuss the meaning of these phrases from the discussion. Then use them to complete the information about microfibers. One phrase is used twice.

break down	end up	makes up

Polyester [1]_____ over half of all fabric used by the fashion industry. It is made of plastic, and when we wash our polyester clothes, the plastic begins to [2]_____ into microfibers. Those microfibers [3]_____ in our rivers and oceans, where they're eaten by fish. Ultimately, they [4]_____ back in our bodies.

NOTE-TAKING TIP

When you are listening to a group discussion, remembering who said what can be difficult. To make it easier, make a note of the speakers' names and their roles or titles at the top of your notes. Then, as you are taking notes, write their initials next to the points that they make.

RL: 80–100 billion items clothing/year

B MAIN IDEAS
Listen to the introduction to a panel discussion and complete the notes. 🎧 2.3

Festival of Ideas

Topic: Fast fashion: threats and [1]_____

Panel: SF: Sara Flores – lecturer in fashion [2]_____

YX: Yuan Xu – environmental [3]_____ & author

MT: Megan Turner – [4]_____ journalist & blogger

C MAIN IDEAS
Listen to the discussion. Write the initials of the person who makes each statement. Choose the correct answers to complete the sentences. 🎧 2.4

1. _____ The fashion industry makes **far fewer / a few more / many more** items of clothing now than 20 years ago.

2. _____ **A bit / Most / All** of the water in the Aral Sea has disappeared because of cotton farming.

3. _____ Cotton farming provides jobs for 100 million **shop workers / farmers / factory workers**.

4. _____ Washing **synthetic / natural / synthetic and natural** fabrics causes microfibers to pollute the environment.

5. _____ Most people **know / don't know / know but don't care** about the environmental costs of fast fashion.

6. _____ It's estimated that the fashion industry will be three times bigger in **less than 20 years / about 30 years / about 50 years**.

LISTENING SKILL   Listen for data and take notes

When you listen to a lecture, you may need to write down data in the form of numbers. You can use numerals and abbreviations. Here are some common types of data and examples of notes.

Numbers   two thousand (2K), fifteen million (15 mil.), eighteen billion (18 bil.), two trillion (2 tril.)

The world population is about 7.5 billion people.   *world pop. = 7.5 bil.*

Area   nine square feet (9 sq. ft.), four square miles (4 sq. mi.)

Lake Vostok in Antarctica is about 5,000 square miles.   *Lake Vostok = 5K sq. mi.*

Volume   ten gallons (10 gal.)

One person uses about 80 gallons of water a day.   *water = 80 gal./day/person*

Weight   two-thousand pounds (2,000 lb.), one ton (1 tn.)

Two-thousand pounds equals one ton.   *2,000 lb. = 1 tn.*

D DETAILS Listen again and write the numbers. Use numerals and abbreviations. Check your answers with a partner. 🎧2.4

1. How big is the fashion industry in terms of dollars? _____

2. How many items of clothing are manufactured globally every year? _____

3. How big was the Aral Sea in the past? _____

    How much water is left? _____

4. How many farmers around the world work in the cotton industry? _____

5. How much water is required to grow the cotton for one pair of jeans? _____

6. How much polyester is used by the fashion industry each year? _____

7. How much insect-killing chemicals does growing cotton use globally? _____

8. How many items of clothing might be manufactured per year by 2050? _____

CRITICAL THINKING   Use current trends to imagine the future

Data doesn't tell us about only the past and present. It also gives us a chance to imagine what will happen in the future if current trends continue. When you look at a graph, imagine what will happen at a particular point in the future if the trend in the graph continues (e.g., 10 years from now).

If current trends continue, by 2035 the average consumer will own 200 items of clothing.

Bundles of old clothing in a recycling center

REFLECT Estimate the impact of fashion trends.

Work with a partner.

1. Look at the graphs. Discuss what the data in each one shows.

2. Use the data to imagine the future impact of each trend. Which trend could cause the most serious challenges? Explain.

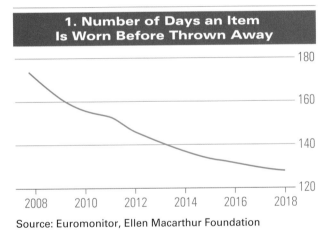

1. Number of Days an Item Is Worn Before Thrown Away

Source: Euromonitor, Ellen Macarthur Foundation

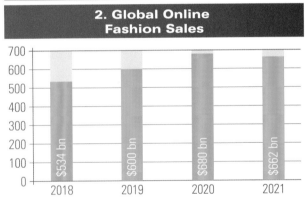

2. Global Online Fashion Sales

Source: Statista, 2018

3. Number of Items of Clothing Sold

Source: Euromonitor, Ellen Macarthur Foundation

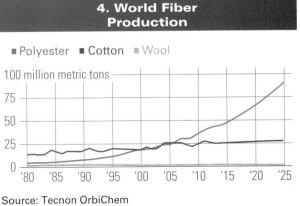

4. World Fiber Production

■ Polyester ■ Cotton ■ Wool

100 million metric tons

Source: Tecnon OrbiChem

PREPARE TO WATCH

A VOCABULARY Listen to the words in bold. Then choose the correct meaning of each word. 🎧 2.5

1. The "slow fashion" **approach** involves manufacturing small amounts of high-quality clothes.

   a. a difficult situation   b. a way to deal with a situation   c. an idea

2. In some countries, people **discard** up to 70 pounds (32 kilograms) of old clothes per person, per year.

   a. give up   b. hold onto   c. throw away

3. Every time we wash synthetic clothes, microfibers break off. Some end up in the food we eat. Microfibers are not **edible**, so it's a problem when they are found in food.

   a. safe to eat   b. safe to touch   c. safe to smell

4. The fashion industry **generates** more greenhouse gas than the airline industry and the shipping industry together.

   a. buys   b. uses   c. makes

5. One reason people buy so many new clothes is because their **peers** do.

   a. people of similar age and social position   b. people in your family   c. people who you admire

6. Fast fashion is very **profitable**. The largest companies can make around $30,000 a minute.

   a. spending too much money   b. bringing in more money than is spent   c. not having enough money to cover costs

7. Enough clothes to fill 60 garbage trucks are burned or sent to landfills every minute. Most people agree that this is **simply** too much.

   a. of course   b. just   c. at least

8. Growing cotton requires a lot of water. Some companies are trying to **tackle** this problem with new fabrics that need less water.

   a. solve   b. ignore   c. make worse

9. The fabric-dying process (changing the color of fabric) uses tons of **toxic** chemicals.

   a. colorful   b. dangerous to your health   c. safe to use

10. The largest fashion companies have a **turnover** of over $20 billion a year, which makes them extremely successful.

    a. money a business spends   b. money a business needs   c. money a business makes

B PERSONALIZE Which facts in activity A are the most surprising or interesting to you? Discuss with a partner.

Brainstorming is the process of coming up with ideas, for example, to solve a problem. It is often done with a group of people. If you take part in a brainstorming session, the "golden rule" is to accept what other people say and not to criticize. All ideas should be considered.

REFLECT Brainstorm solutions to issues in fast fashion.

Before you watch a video about new approaches to the challenges of fast fashion, reread the sentences in activity A.

1. Choose one issue from activity A and write it below.
2. Take two minutes alone to brainstorm ways to solve the problem. Write them in the chart.
3. In a small group, brainstorm solutions to the issues the group members chose.
4. Choose the best idea for each issue and share it with the class.

Issue	Solutions
▶	▶
	▶
	▶

The Neonyt Fashion Show in Berlin, Germany, features clothing from sustainable fashion labels.

A NEW APPROACH

The clothing storage area for ThredUp, an online thrift store, Phoenix, Arizona, USA

A PHRASES TO KNOW Work with a partner. Discuss the meaning of these phrases from the video. Then take turns answering the questions.

1. What was the last paid online service that you **signed up** for?

2. Many things can be **turned into** fabric, for example, cotton and plastic. What else can be turned into fabric to make clothes?

3. Can you think of some companies that are trying to help the environment, reduce waste, and **turn** things **around**?

B MAIN IDEAS Watch the video about companies that are trying to solve problems in the fashion industry. Match each company to the correct problem and solution. ▶ 2.1

| a. YCloset | b. By Rotation | c. Tonlé | d. EcoAlf | e. Patagonia |

Problems

1. _____ The environment is polluted with discarded plastics that end up in the ocean.

2. _____ Clothing factories produce a lot of waste fabric.

3. _____ People don't repair or recycle their old clothes.

4. _____ People buy too many clothes.

5. _____ Many clothes are bought but never worn.

Solutions

6. _____ Offer a repair service and recycling options.

7. _____ Rent clothes to customers instead of selling them.

8. _____ Allow customers to rent clothes to each other.

9. _____ Use the fabric that other factories throw away.

10. _____ Use waste plastic in the sea to make fabric.

C DETAILS Watch the video again and complete each sentence with two or three words. ▶ 2.1

1. The only industry that is more polluting than fashion is _____.

2. When you have finished with your YCloset clothes, you simply _____ to be cleaned and rented again.

3. The By Rotation approach is called _____ rental.

4. Most of the chemicals that Tonlé uses to dye clothes _____.

5. EcoAlf removes over 150 _____ from the ocean every year.

6. Patagonia charges customers a _____ for repairing their clothes, or they will recycle them.

D Discuss the questions with a partner.

1. Which solution in the video do you think will have the biggest impact on the fashion industry and the environment?

2. Are there any companies you would or wouldn't use? Which ones? Explain.

You are going to take part in a meeting. The purpose of the meeting is to come up with a plan on how to save a fashion company. Use the ideas, skills, and vocabulary from the unit.

E MODEL Listen to the meeting. Choose the correct answers. 🎧 2.6

1. The purpose of the meeting is to **find an approach / brainstorm ideas / explain how** to save the company.

2. Breona thinks the biggest problem is not **being friendly to customers / being friendly to the environment / listening to customers**.

3. Breona suggests using **more / fewer / no** synthetic fabrics.

4. Breona thinks that customers will **understand / not like / not notice** a price increase if it means protecting the environment.

5. Carlos suggests taking **a different / the same / a typical** approach to solve their problem.

6. Carlos suggests **repairing / recycling / buying back** their customers' old clothes.

7. Carlos thinks an advantage is that their competitors **buy back / don't buy back / want to buy back** clothes from customers.

8. Dimitri thinks Carlos's idea is too **unusual / expensive / detailed**.

9. Dimitri thinks the biggest problem is that their clothes are too **cheap / old-fashioned / expensive**.

10. Dimitri suggests using **more / less / no** synthetic fabric to cut costs, be more profitable, and increase turnover.

Designers meet in Montreal, Quebec, Canada.

SPEAKING SKILL Acknowledge other arguments

In a meeting, it is good to respond positively to what other people say, even when they are disagreeing with you. A good strategy is to a) say that the other person has a good point, b) repeat the point, and c) offer an alternative opinion.

F APPLY Listen to the excerpts from the meeting. Complete each response with the sentences from columns a, b, and c that you hear. 🎧 2.7

a. Say that the other person has a good point.	b. Repeat the point.	c. Offer an alternative opinion.
▸ That's true.	▸ It would be something new.	▸ But it's still possible.
▸ I see your point.	▸ Price is important.	▸ But it would also be expensive.
▸ Carlos is right.	▸ It isn't easy.	▸ But it's not everything.

1. **Dimitri:** We can't forget that our customers want cheap clothes.

   Breona: a. _____ b. _____

   c. _____ Customers want to help the environment.

2. **Breona:** I'm not sure about that idea. It could get very complicated.

   Carlos: a. _____ b. _____

   c. _____ We can be the first.

3. **Alice:** Dimitri, what's your opinion?

   Dimitri: a. _____ b. _____

   c. _____ We need to cut costs.

G APPLY Complete the conversations. Then take turns reading them with a partner.

1. **A:** Renting clothes is the future of fashion.

   B: I think people prefer to buy clothes. They don't want to rent them.

   A: _____

2. **A:** We all buy too many clothes.

   B: But the clothing industry creates jobs for many people.

   A: _____

3. **A:** Slow fashion is the future.

   B: But slow fashion is expensive.

   A: _____

GRAMMAR   Noun clauses

A noun clause is a group of words (with a subject and a verb) that together act as a noun. A noun clause can be in the subject or object position in a sentence.

That

A noun clause can begin with *that* or *the fact that*. *The fact that* is often used when the noun clause starts the sentence.

> **The fact that our competitors don't do this** is important.
> We can't forget **that our customers want cheap clothes**.

Wh- question words

A noun clause can begin with a question word such as *how, who, what,* or *why*. *Wh*-word noun clauses follow statement word order, not question word order.

> We need to figure out **how we make our clothes affordable**.
> NOT: *We need to figure out ~~how do we make our clothes affordable.~~*

Whoever, whenever, whatever

When the noun clause begins with *whoever, whenever,* or *whatever*, the meaning is "anyone, any time, or anything."

> We aim to give our customers **whatever they want**.

H GRAMMAR Underline the noun clause in each sentence.

1. What I suggest is a different approach.

2. I know that our clothes will be more expensive.

3. I'm interested in what our competitors are doing.

4. Whoever thought of that idea is very clever.

5. I'm really unhappy about the fact that he's not here.

6. Let's not forget why we are here.

7. They can buy whatever they want when they go shopping.

8. Did you know that you need 2,000 silkworms to make a silk dress?

I GRAMMAR Replace the underlined noun with a noun clause. Use the sentence in parentheses to make the noun clause.

1. I'm only interested in <u>one thing</u>. (How much money do we make?)

   I'm only interested in how much money we make.

2. <u>That</u> is surprising. (She doesn't care about fashion.)

   _____

3. We need to ask him <u>a question</u>. (What does he want to do?)

   _____

4. I will help you to get <u>it</u>. (Whatever you want is fine.)

_____

5. <u>That</u> is difficult to understand. (Why do they want that?)

_____

6. I like <u>that</u>. (You always tell the truth.)

_____

7. We need to research <u>it</u>. (How did they do that?)

_____

8. We know <u>it</u>. (Sneakers are very popular with teens.)

_____

J GRAMMAR Complete the sentences. Then compare answers with a partner.

1. What I don't understand about fashion is why _____.

2. I buy new clothes whenever _____.

3. I like the fact that your clothes _____.

4. Can you explain to me how _____?

PRONUNCIATION   Intonation in questions and statements 📢2.8

Intonation is the pitch of the voice. In English, the voice moves more than in many other languages, and most of the movement happens on a stressed focus word. The focus word is usually the last content word in a statement or question. In general, intonation falls on the focus word at the end of statements and *wh-* questions. It rises on the focus word at the end of *yes/no* questions.

*I'm not sure what to **suggest**.*

*What is he planning to **do** now?*

*Are you planning to **leave** it here?*

K PRONUNCIATION Listen and underline the focus word. Then draw a ↓ if the voice falls and a ↑ if the voice rises. Then take turns asking the questions with a partner. 📢2.9

1. What should I wear? _____

2. Should I wear this? _____

3. I like what you're wearing today. _____

4. Do you like her jeans? _____

5. I'm not sure what to do now. _____

6. Do you know what to do? _____

7. I think I know what to say about it. _____

8. I think it's time to go. _____

L PLAN Read the situation. In groups of four, decide on your roles for the meeting to help save your company. Use the chart to prepare your role. Write what you want to say in the meeting.

Your company, *Fabulous Future Fashions*, makes clothing for 16- to 25-year olds. Recently, customers have been criticizing the company on social media for being too expensive, having poor quality, and not being environmentally friendly. Sales are going down, and the company is in danger of failing.

▸ CEO: leads the meeting, wants to hear opinions and makes the final decision
▸ Head of Finance: wants to cut costs and sell more
▸ Head of Marketing: wants to take a more environmentally friendly approach
▸ Head of Production: wants to change but is worried about the cost and difficulty

Biggest problems	Ideas for change	Reasons for idea

LEARNING TIP

Make sure people in a meeting understand the purpose of the meeting and what is expected of them. You can say things such as:

So, the purpose of today's meeting is . . .

I'd like everyone to contribute.

M PRACTICE Hold your group meeting. Listen to each other and acknowledge what others say. Together agree on a plan to change the business.

N UNIT TASK Present your plan to the class. As you listen to other groups, take notes in your notebook. As a class, decide which plans of action would be the most successful.

REFLECT

A Check (✓) the Reflect activities you can do and the academic skills you can use.

☐ rank the pros and cons of fast fashion

☐ estimate the impact of fashion trends

☐ brainstorm solutions to issues in fast fashion

☐ make a plan to save a fashion company

☐ listen for data and take notes

☐ acknowledge other arguments

☐ noun clauses

☐ use current trends to imagine the future

B Write the vocabulary words from the unit in the correct column. Add any other words that you learned. Circle words you still need to practice.

NOUN	VERB	ADJECTIVE	ADVERB & OTHER

C Reflect on the ideas in the unit as you answer these questions.

1. What is the most important thing you learned in this unit?

_____

_____

2. Who do you think is responsible for making the fashion industry more environmentally friendly?

_____

_____

3. Will you change your clothes-shopping habits in the future?

_____

_____

A man enjoys the warm waters of Iceland's Blue Lagoon.

CONNECT TO THE TOPIC

1. Look at the photo. Have you ever had an experience like this?

2. In what ways have washing habits changed over time?

PREPARE TO LISTEN

A VOCABULARY Listen to the words. Match the words with the definitions. ⏹3.1

1. _____ **attain** (v)   a.   to make an illness or a disease go away

2. _____ **cure** (v)   b.   easy to understand or do

3. _____ **historically** (adv)   c.   to give medical care to someone

4. _____ **hygiene** (n)   d.   to repeatedly move your fingers or hand over something

5. _____ **medical** (adj)   e.   the ways of keeping things clean to prevent disease

6. _____ **norm** (n)   f.   to achieve after a lot of work

7. _____ **rub** (v)   g.   to produce water through your skin when you are hot

8. _____ **straightforward** (adj) h.   the usual, normal way that something is done

9. _____ **sweat** (v)   i.   related to medicine and doctors

10. _____ **treat** (v)   j.   related to history or past events

B VOCABULARY Complete each sentence with a word from activity A.

1. Some people make their own shampoo. It's very _____ and easy to do. All you need is water, the right kind of soap, and sweet-smelling oils.

2. Many people use honey or salt water to _____ a sore throat. It doesn't make it completely better, but it helps.

3. Ancient Egyptians used a "chewstick," which was a kind of toothbrush, and soap to clean themselves. Even 5,000 years ago, people knew that good _____ prevents health problems.

4. We usually _____ when we are hot from exercise or the weather. It helps to control our body's temperature.

5. _____, attitudes toward handwashing have changed a lot. For example, just 150 years ago, doctors in hospitals rarely washed their hands.

6. The leaves of the aloe vera plant contain a gel. You can _____ this gel into your skin to make your skin softer.

7. In hospitals, the goal is to be completely clean. It's not an easy goal to _____, but it's essential for public health.

8. In the past, doctors used leeches (small animals that suck blood) for all kinds of _____ problems. Believe it or not, leeches are still used in some situations in hospitals today.

9. A few hundred years ago, getting your barber or hairdresser to pull your teeth was the _____. There were no specialized dentists, so it was the only option.

10. There are at least 160 different forms of the cold virus. This is why scientists still haven't been able to _____ the common cold.

C PERSONALIZE Do you agree or disagree with these statements? Explain your answers to a partner.

1. You get the best **medical** advice from a doctor.
2. It's healthy to **sweat** a lot when you exercise.
3. It takes a lot of work to **attain** a high level of **hygiene** in the home.

REFLECT   Consider how ideas about cleanliness change over time.

You are going to listen to a lecture about the history of hygiene. Discuss these questions with a partner.

1. What are the personal hygiene habits of people in your country (e.g., shower once a day, clean shirt every day)?
2. In what ways do you think those habits have changed over the last 100 years?
3. Is there a tradition of using public baths in your country (e.g., sauna, bathhouse)? If so, how long has that tradition existed?

Children washing their hands before a school meal, Chiquimula, Guatemala

3,500 YEARS OF HYGIENE

A PREDICT Look at the timeline. What kind of information do you think you might learn in the lecture?

B Listen to the lecture and write the correct dates on the timeline. 🎧 3.2

C MAIN IDEAS Choose the main idea.

    a. Soap has always been an important part of personal hygiene in every culture.

    b. Ideas of hygiene change according to time, place, and culture.

    c. Since 1500 BCE, different cultures often have similar standards of hygiene.

D DETAILS Listen again. Write T for *True* or F for *False*. Then correct the false sentences. 🎧 3.2

    1. _____ People in ancient Egypt used soap for personal hygiene and to treat skin diseases.

    2. _____ People in ancient Rome used soap and a metal tool to get clean.

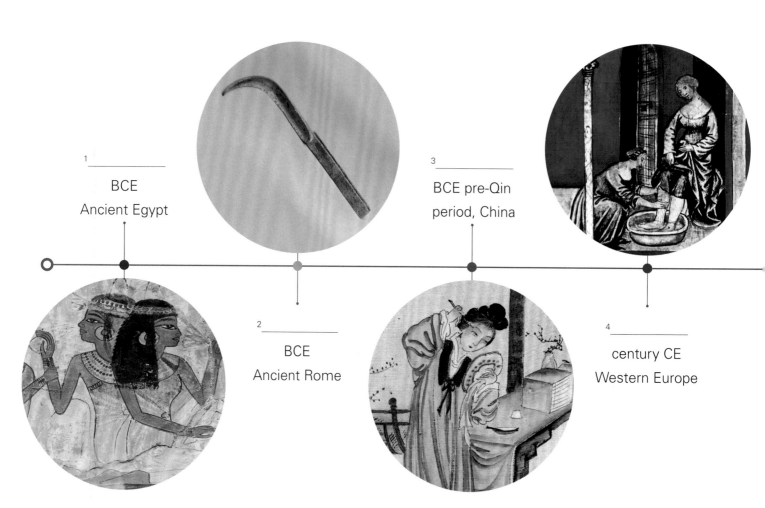

1 _____
BCE
Ancient Egypt

3 _____
BCE pre-Qin
period, China

2 _____
BCE
Ancient Rome

4 _____
century CE
Western Europe

3. _____ During the pre-Qin period in China, people bathed regularly and washed their hands many times a day to prevent illness.

4. _____ People in 14th-century Europe thought that water cured diseases.

5. _____ The Aztec people in Mexico bathed regularly.

6. _____ Public bath houses, called *sentō*, were very popular during the Edo period in Japan.

7. _____ In the early 20th century, people in the United States bathed several times a week.

E PHRASES TO KNOW Work with a partner. Discuss the meaning of the phrases from the lecture. Then answer the questions.

1. According to the lecture, people **came up with** strange ideas about the causes of disease. What were some of these ideas?

2. Visitors **were taken aback by** how clean the local population was. Where was this? What did visitors observe that was so surprising?

3. The practice of bathing with others really **took off** during the Edo period. Can you explain why this happened?

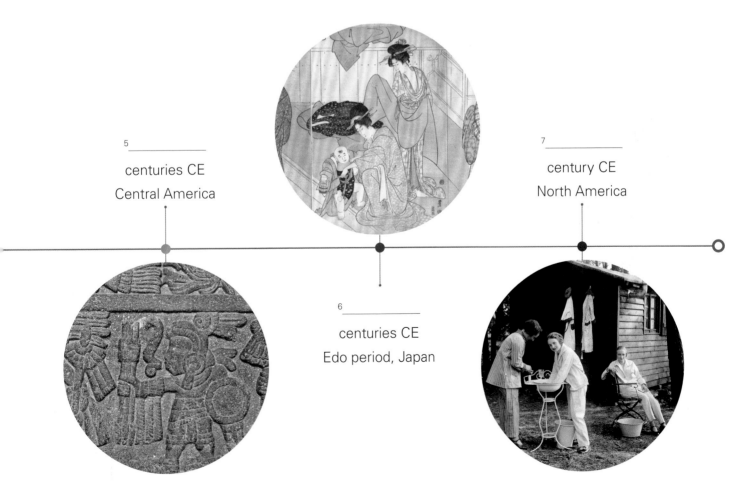

5 _____
centuries CE
Central America

6 _____
centuries CE
Edo period, Japan

7 _____
century CE
North America

LISTENING SKILL Listen for sources of information

When giving a talk, speakers often mention the source of their information. The source might be an expert, a witness, a book, or other documents. Recognizing the source of information is a useful skill because it helps you determine how valid the information is.

Listen for these phrases which are used to introduce sources of information. (Sources are in blue.)

According to Professor Pinker . . .   The Ebers Papyrus **shows that** . . .

We **know from** reports **that** . . .   Witnesses at the time **tell us that** . . .

A document written at the time **refers to** . . .   Ancient documents **prove that** . . .

F APPLY Listen to an excerpt from the lecture. Complete the sentences. Then underline the sources and the phrases that introduce them. 🎧 3.3

1. In ancient Egypt, according to the *Ebers Papyrus*, people _____

   a. had many different skin diseases.

   b. used soap for hundreds of different reasons.

   c. used soap to stay clean and healthy.

2. In ancient Rome, writers of the time tell us that people _____

   a. didn't like water.

   b. sweated as part of the cleaning process.

   c. used oil and dust after bathing.

3. We know from the *Huangdi Neijing* that ancient Chinese people _____

   a. understood that hygiene prevents illness.

   b. enjoyed bathing in rice water.

   c. knew how to cure illnesses.

4. According to the historian Katherine Ashenburg, in the 14th century, women wore perfume _____

   a. because they liked the nice smell.

   b. to cover the bad smell of other people.

   c. to keep "bad air" away from them.

5. The Florentine Codex shows that the Aztec people _____

   a. washed their mouths with soap.

   b. washed next to special trees.

   c. used natural soaps and deodorants.

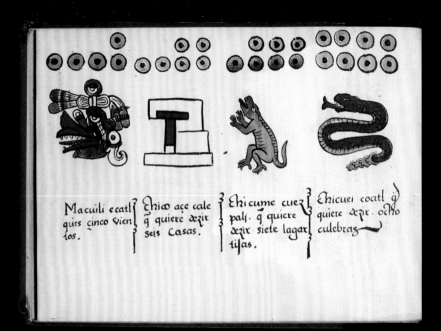

The Florentine Codex is a 16th-century document about the areas now known as Mexico and Central America.

CRITICAL THINKING   Evaluate sources of information

In academic study and everyday life, you need to be able to tell the difference between reliable and unreliable sources of information. Well-known experts and authentic documents are more trustworthy and reliable than unknown bloggers or websites. For example, in the listening, Professor Bashar refers to a well-known historian. Consequently, you can assume that her information is accurate.

> ***According to historian Katherine Ashenburg***, *in the 14th century, women began to wear perfume so that they wouldn't notice the smell of other people.*

G APPLY Listen and evaluate the speaker's sources. Complete the chart. 🎧 3.4

	Source	The speaker's source . . .	
		is probably reliable.	might not be reliable.
1.			
2.			
3.			

REFLECT   Evaluate sources of information from the past and present.

Discuss these questions with a partner.

1. What are the characteristics of reliable sources of information?

2. What current sources of information do you trust or not trust? Think about newspapers, websites, podcasts, etc. Explain with examples.

PREPARE TO WATCH

A **VOCABULARY** Listen to the words in bold. Then read the sentences. Choose the correct meaning for the words. ▶ 3.5

1. The first advertisements were painted on walls or printed on paper. Nowadays, **advertisers** have more options, for example, online, TV, and social media.

   a. people who make ads
   b. people who see ads
   c. people who make products in ads

2. A common **belief** in the past was that bad air around lakes could make you ill.

   a. idea
   b. hope
   c. doubt

3. Ads often **claim** that a product is very different from everything else, but that's not usually true.

   a. state
   b. recognize
   c. warn

4. The **concept** of cleanliness has changed a lot over time. Just 100 years ago, people believed that they were clean if they bathed once a week in dirty water.

   a. experience
   b. feeling
   c. idea

5. Smallpox is a **deadly** disease. In the 20th century, 300 million people died from it.

   a. common
   b. likely to kill you
   c. painful

6. Most cleaning products come in bottles that are **designed** to stop young children from opening them.

   a. covered in pictures
   b. made from plastic
   c. made in a certain way

7. Ibn Sina, a scholar born 1,000 years ago, was the first to discover that **germs** caused disease and illness.

   a. tiny dead things that float in the air
   b. tiny things that kill you
   c. tiny living things that make you sick

8. In the 19th century, 50 percent of people died from **infection** after an operation.

   a. a disease caused by germs
   b. a cut in the skin
   c. a kind of medicine

9. Before a new medicine can be sold, it goes through a lot of testing. The first **phase** of testing is usually in a laboratory. The last phase is tests on humans.

   a. goal
   b. a step in a process
   c. experiment

10. Cholera is a deadly disease that is **spread** through dirty water or dirty food. Doctors can cure it, but many people around the world still die from it every year.

    a. makes you feel better
    b. travels from one person to another
    c. lives in a place

B PERSONALIZE Discuss these questions with a partner.

1. Do you agree that **advertisers** will say anything to make you buy their products? If you agree, give an example.

2. How do most popular trends **spread** these days?

REFLECT   Explain how advertising has influenced hygiene and health.

You are going to watch a video about how advertising has impacted hygiene. Read the statements and write A if you *agree* or D if you *disagree*. Discuss your answers in a small group.

_____ Ads for sugary drinks and snacks cause unhealthy eating habits.

_____ Ads featuring sports stars encourage people to have a healthier lifestyle.

_____ Attractive models in ads make us want to be healthier and more attractive.

_____ Ads for cleaning products improve standards of hygiene in society.

Ho Chi Minh City, Vietnam

WATCH & SPEAK

WHEN ADVERTISERS FIRST FOUGHT GERMS

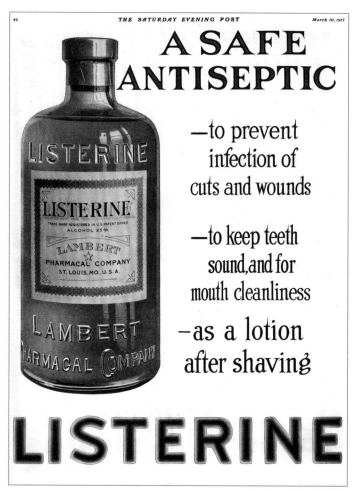

A PREVIEW Look at the ads. Discuss the questions with a partner.

1. What is each advertisement for?

2. When do you think each one was made?

3. How have advertisements changed since then?

B PHRASES TO KNOW Match the phrases from the video with the definitions.

a. believed it	b. make money	c. were enthusiastic about

1. _____ When advertisers realized that they could use fear to sell products, they **jumped on** the idea and used it in a lot of different ads.

2. _____ When people started seeing social media stars using certain products, they totally **bought it** and didn't realize that the stars were being paid.

3. _____ Some advertisers don't care whether the things they say in the ads are true or not. They just want to **make a buck**.

C MAIN IDEAS Watch the video. Choose the main idea. ▶ 3.1

    a. Advertising helped improve public health by selling new furniture and cleaning products.

    b. Advertising didn't improve public health, but it sold a lot of furniture and cleaning products.

    c. Advertising made public health worse by selling cleaning products that didn't work.

D MAIN IDEAS Watch the video again. Write T for *True* or F for *False*. ▶ 3.1

1. _____ It was easy for 19th-century Americans to stay clean.

2. _____ Infectious diseases started to increase in number because of germs.

3. _____ Germ theory was quickly accepted by the general public.

4. _____ Advertisers used germ theory to sell new products.

5. _____ Science showed that germs could be passed from person to person.

6. _____ Advertisers began to advertise carpets and rugs because they were cleaner.

7. _____ Advertisers began to advertise products to clean furniture.

8. _____ Advertisers used Dr. Lister's fame to sell personal hygiene products.

E DETAILS Check (✓) the answers. More than one answer may be correct.

1. Why was it hard for Americans in the 19th century to attain the same cleanliness as now?

    a. _____ They didn't have water from a faucet.

    b. _____ They didn't have a lot of cleaning products.

    c. _____ They didn't enjoy washing and cleaning.

2. Why did it take a long time for germ theory to be accepted by ordinary people?

    a. _____ People couldn't see germs, so they didn't believe they existed.

    b. _____ Advertisers told people that germs didn't exist.

    c. _____ People thought that germs only existed in toilets.

3. Who were the strongest supporters of germ theory in the 1880s?

    a. _____ Doctors and scientists who studied germ theory

    b. _____ People who lived in big cities

    c. _____ Advertisers who wanted to sell products such as toilets

4. What sort of furniture did advertisers try to sell, and why?

    a. _____ Velvet chairs because they were more comfortable

    b. _____ Wicker chairs because they were easier to clean

    c. _____ Rugs and carpets because you could clean them outside

5. For what purposes did advertisers sell Listerine?

    a. _____ To clean furniture

    b. _____ To prevent illness

    c. _____ To improve your social life

PRONUNCIATION Word stress 🎧3.6

Words with suffixes

The stress often depends on the suffix. For example, words ending in *-ic*, *-al*, *-ive*, or *-ion* usually have the stress on the syllable immediately before the suffix.

ex-**pens**-ive   sci-en-**tif**-ic   in-**fec**-tion

Nouns and verbs

When a word has two syllables or more, one syllable always carries the main stress. With two-syllable nouns, it is often the first syllable. With two-syllable verbs, it is often the second syllable.

Nouns:	**pro**-duct	**con**-cept	**toi**-let
Verbs:	a-**ttain**	in-**fect**	be-**lieve**

Stress shift

The stress often shifts from one syllable to another when the form or meaning of the word changes.

hy-giene (n) ➔ hy-**gien**-ic (adj)   **pho**-to-graph (n, thing) ➔ pho-**to**-gra-pher (n, person)

F PRONUNCIATION Check (✓) the correct pronunciation of these words. Then listen and repeat. 🎧3.7

1. a. _____ **an**-ti-sep-tic   b. _____ an-ti-**sep**-tic

2. a. _____ his-**tor**-i-cal   b. _____ his-tor-i-**cal**

3. a. _____ **pro**-tec-tion   b. _____ pro-**tec**-tion

4. a. _____ mi-cro-**sco**-pic   b. _____ **mi**-cro-sco-pic

5. a. _____ **cre**-a-tive   b. _____ cre-**a**-tive

G PRONUNCIATION Listen and circle the stressed syllable in the underlined nouns and verbs. Then listen and repeat. 🎧3.8

1. It con-tains many ways to cure health pro-blems.

2. They used a piece of me-tal to re-move the dust from their skin.

3. It is important to pre-vent ill-ness.

4. The document re-fers to the natural pro-ducts that they used.

H PRONUNCIATION Look at the underlined words and circle the stressed syllable in each. Then listen and repeat. 🎧3.9

1. Are you a good pre-sen-ter? Do you like giving pre-sen-ta-tions?

2. Have you ever seen an ad-ver-tise-ment that was ad-ver-tis-ing beauty products for children?

3. Are you a tech-ni-cal person? Do you like working with new tech-nol-o-gy?

4. Do you have a strong i-mag-in-a-tion? Did you have an i-mag-in-a-ry friend as a child?

Compare ads from different times in history.

You are going to give a presentation about the differences between two ads for a product, one from the past and one from the present. You will explain what each shows about society at the time it was created. Use the ideas, vocabulary, and skills from the unit.

I MODEL Listen to a student describing two ads. Take notes in the chart. Then compare your notes with a partner. 🔊3.10

	Old magazine ad	Current social media ad	Reason for differences
The first thing you notice			
The images			
The text			
The advertisers			

dunia_hassankumar • **Following**   ...

Do you want to have the smoothest, loveliest skin in the world? Check out Salayam's new soap. It's made with natural ingredients and is cruelty-free. 👍 I use it every day. #soap #skincare #crueltyfree #beauty #glow #skincareroutine #freshfaces

SPEAKING SKILL   Refer to and describe visuals

When using visuals in a presentation, follow these guidelines.

1. Be sure that everyone can see the visual.
2. Don't talk to the visual; talk to the audience.
3. When you have finished talking about the visual, take it away.

Use these phrases to refer to visuals and to point out different aspects.

Take a look at . . .	*Notice . . . / You'll notice . . .*
I'd like you to/Now take a look at . . .	*It shows . . .*
The first thing you'll notice is . . .	*As you can see . . .*

J APPLY Choose one of the ads below and describe it to a partner.

1. Where would you see this ad?
2. What is the purpose of this ad?
3. Who does the advertiser want to appeal to?
4. What do you see first?
5. What do you notice about the ad?
6. Is it an effective form of advertising? Explain.

GRAMMAR Reduced adjective clauses

Remember: An adjective clause is a dependent clause that gives more information about a noun. Subject adjective clauses begin with a relative pronoun, such as *who*, *which*, *that*, or *whose*. A verb follows the relative pronoun.

> Take a look at the <u>text</u> **that describes the benefits of using the soap**.

We can reduce or shorten some subject adjective clauses. To do this, take out the relative pronoun, the verb *be* (if the clause has one), and use the *-ing* form of the main verb.

> Take a look at the text ~~that describes~~ **describing the benefits of using the soap**.
> The number of people ~~who used~~ **using public baths** increased.
> He was looking for the document ~~that was~~ **sitting on the printer**.

If the verb is in the passive voice, take out the relative pronoun and the verb *be*.

> Photos ~~that are~~ **shared digitally** cost nothing.

K GRAMMAR Underline the adjective clause in each sentence. Then check (✓) the four sentences where the adjective clause can be reduced.

1. _____ The man who is cleaning the dishes in the ad looks very unhappy.

2. _____ The sofa that the family is sitting on is very old-fashioned.

3. _____ Social media stars who are followed by a lot of people are often paid to post about a product.

4. _____ The bottle that she is holding contains an expensive perfume.

5. _____ Advertisers used to make many wild promises that consumers believed.

6. _____ All magazines now rely on the money that is earned from advertising.

7. _____ Almost half the people who saw the online advertisement clicked on it.

8. _____ The ads are aimed at children whose parents want to buy them a present.

L GRAMMAR Rewrite the four sentences that you checked (✓) in activity K with reduced adjective clauses.

1. _____

2. _____

3. _____

4. _____

M PLAN Go online and find two ads for similar products, one old and the other modern. Print the ads out before the next lesson or ensure that you can show them digitally. Use the questions below to plan your presentation. Make notes in your notebook.

Introduction
- ▸ What is the first thing that you notice about each ad?

Images
- ▸ What do the images in each ad show?
- ▸ What are the differences in size and style?
- ▸ What do the images want to make you feel?
- ▸ What might be the reasons for differences in the ads?

Text
- ▸ How would you summarize the text in each ad?
- ▸ What are the differences in length and style of the text?
- ▸ Who seems to be the writer of the text, and who are they talking to?
- ▸ What might be the reasons for these differences?

Conclusion
- ▸ What do the differences in the ads tell us about changes in advertising and society?

N PRACTICE Practice giving your presentation to a partner. Think about the language that you will use to refer to and describe the visuals.

O UNIT TASK Work in a small group. Present your two ads. As you listen to other students, take notes. Which ads did you like the best? Explain.

	Student 1	Student 2	Student 3
The first thing that you notice			
The difference in images			
The difference in text			
The conclusions			

REFLECT

A Check (✓) the Reflect activities you can do and the academic skills you can use.

- ☐ consider how ideas about cleanliness change over time
- ☐ evaluate sources of information from the past and present
- ☐ explain how advertising has influenced hygiene and health
- ☐ compare ads for products from different times in history

- ☐ listen for sources of information
- ☐ refer to and describe visuals
- ☐ reduced adjective clauses
- ☐ evaluate sources of information

B Write the vocabulary words from the unit in the correct column. Add any other words that you learned. Circle words you still need to practice.

NOUN	VERB	ADJECTIVE	ADVERB & OTHER

C Reflect on the ideas in the unit as you answer these questions.

1. What facts about the history of hygiene have you learned in this unit?

_____

_____

2. How do you think hygiene habits might change in the future with new technology?

_____

_____

3. What is the most important thing you learned in this unit?

_____

_____

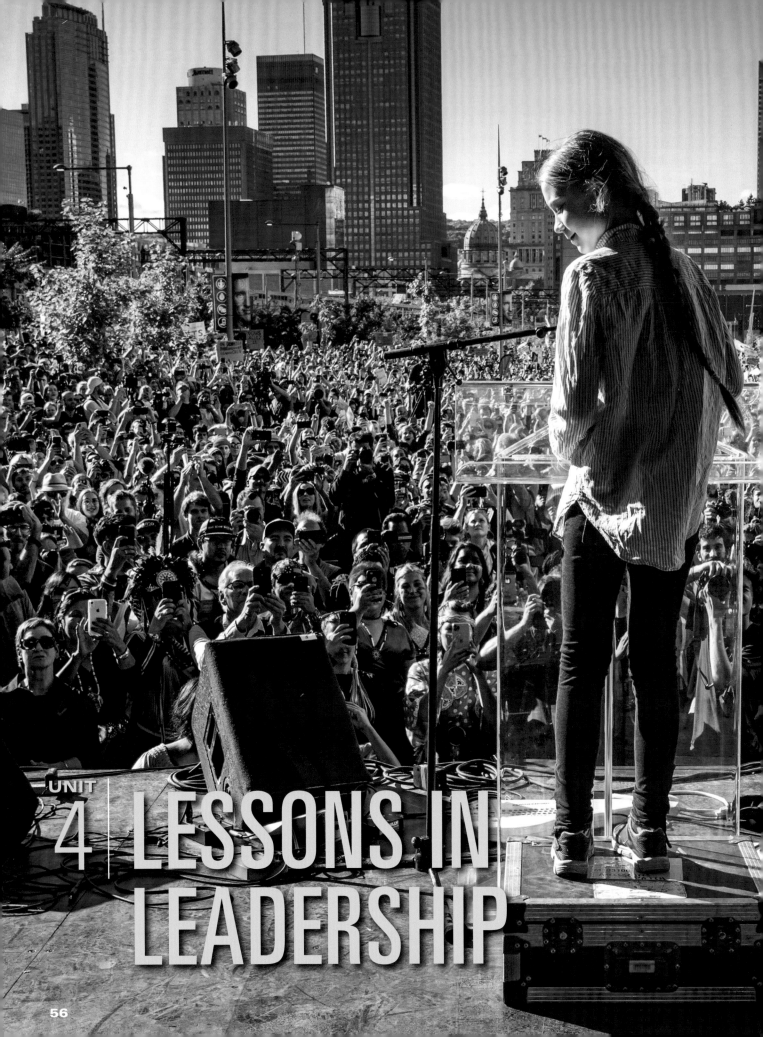

LESSONS IN LEADERSHIP

Swedish activist, Greta Thunberg,
Montreal, Quebec, Canada

CONNECT TO THE TOPIC

1. What is happening in the photo? How do you think it relates to the unit title?

2. What qualities make a leader effective?

PREPARE TO WATCH

A VOCABULARY Listen to the words. Then read the definitions. Complete the sentences with the correct form of the words. ⏯ 4.1

---

bond (n) a connection
constantly (adv) repeatedly or all the time
drought (n) a long period of time with little or no rain
function (n) a purpose or responsibility; job
impact (n) effect
initiate (v) to begin or start
observe (v) to watch carefully
predator (n) an animal that eats other animals
role (n) a job someone or something has in a given situation
threat (n) a person or thing that may cause harm

---

1. A good team leader always _____ the members of their team closely in order to judge their performance and tell them how to improve.

2. Good team leaders _____ support the people on their team. They should never stop trying to help team members to do their jobs.

3. The manager of a sports team should have a very strong _____ with the players on the team. The players should like the manager and feel close to him or her.

4. Most of us play different _____ in our lives, such as student, friend, sibling, employee, or manager.

5. During a natural disaster, such as an earthquake or a _____, people will automatically look for a leader to help them.

6. Poor leaders try to divide and rule. They _____ arguments between different people so that those people will not focus on their bad leadership.

7. A new manager often has a big _____ on a professional sports team. For example, she may cause the team to play better, at least in the short term.

8. In ant colonies, the queen is usually thought of as the leader, but she doesn't tell the other ants what to do. Her _____ is simply to lay eggs.

9. Killer whales are the top _____ in the ocean. No animals, apart from humans, hunt killer whales.

10. Weak leaders see other people with good ideas as a _____. They may try to make these people look bad.

B PERSONALIZE Discuss the questions with a partner.

1. What do you think is the most important **function** of a leader?

2. How can a poor leader **impact** a group or organization?

C Do you think these statements are true or false? Write T for *True* or F for *False*. Then listen and correct the false answers. 🎧 4.2

1. _____ The strongest lion is usually the leader of the group.

2. _____ Female lions do most of the hunting and fighting.

3. _____ Elephants and killer whales almost always have a female leader.

4. _____ Hyenas, a member of the cat family, fight for leadership.

5. _____ The queen bee makes the decisions in a beehive.

REFLECT Consider how animals lead.

You are going to watch a video about leadership in the animal kingdom. With a partner, discuss the advantages and disadvantages of the ways that some animal leaders are chosen.

1. One animal fights the leader and wins leadership of the group.
2. The group decides to accept one animal as the leader.
3. The leadership passes from the leader to the leader's children.
4. There is no leader, and decisions are made by all members of the group together.

European wolves

LEARNING FROM **ANIMALS**

Geese normally migrate during late summer and fall.

A PREDICT Look at the photo. Why do you think birds fly in a V-formation?

B PHRASES TO KNOW With a partner, discuss the meanings of these phrases from the video. Then take turns answering the questions.

1. Do you know anyone who has **taken over** a family business? What was the business?

2. Which animals rarely have to **look out for** predators?

3. When you have a free day and you want to relax, where do you **head for**?

LISTENING SKILL   Infer meaning

Speakers do not always state everything that they want you to take away from a talk. They expect you to infer ideas that have not been said directly. To do this, you have to draw conclusions from what the speaker *does* say and from your own knowledge.

> **Speaker:** *Dolphins do not respond positively to threats. To teach a dolphin a new skill, a trainer uses rewards and praise. He doesn't punish it when it does the wrong thing. This is an important lesson for anyone who wants to be a leader.*

> **You can infer:** To be a good leader, you should use positive techniques, such as rewards and praise, not negative techniques such as punishment.

C MAIN IDEAS Watch the video. What leadership lessons can be inferred from the behavior of these animals? Match. ▶ 4.1

Animal	Leadership lesson you can infer
1. _____ Birds	a. Everyone needs a role that suits their skills.
2. _____ Horses	b. Leaders must use a variety of strategies to stay in charge.
3. _____ Elephants	c. Good leaders don't try to do all the work alone.
4. _____ Wolves	d. Successful leaders have a lot of experience and treat everyone equally.
5. _____ Chimpanzees	e. Having fun with the people you're leading will help create a strong connection.
6. _____ Multiple animal species	f. Experience is important to being a successful leader.

D DETAILS Watch the video again. Write T for *True* or F for *False*. Then correct the false statements. ▶4.1

1. _____ When a goose flaps its wings, it pushes the air behind it upward. This helps the geese behind to fly much farther.

2. _____ Another goose takes over leadership when the previous leader is hungry.

3. _____ Horses are constantly looking out for animals to attack.

4. _____ Horses are not usually good at every role that the herd needs.

5. _____ During the drought in Tanzania, the younger leaders of the elephant groups didn't head for new areas, and the groups didn't do well.

6. _____ Experience taught the older elephant leaders that the drought was very serious, and they needed to move to find food and water.

7. _____ Wolves always howl at the moon alone.

8. _____ For wolves in a group, the function of play is to help them form strong bonds with each other and with their leader.

9. _____ The stronger the chimp, the longer it will stay the leader.

10. _____ Chimp leaders understand the importance of forming bonds with other chimps.

E Discuss these questions with a partner.

1. Do you agree that we can learn important lessons about leadership from animals? If so, which lessons do you think are the most important for leaders to learn?

2. Have you learned anything from animals? Explain.

CRITICAL THINKING   Extend ideas

The ideas that you hear in a lecture can often be applied to new situations or topics. In the video, you heard about lessons that leaders can learn from animals. This idea could be extended to a new topic, such as lessons that *engineers* can learn from animals.

For example, geckos can climb walls easily because of the thousands of tiny elastic hairs on their feet. A team at Stanford University in the United States has extended the idea to create gloves that allow humans to climb vertical glass walls.

Extending an idea will help you to see new possibilities and also to judge whether the idea is a good one.

Gecko

A Stanford engineer climbs a wall using a gecko-inspired device, USA.

Extend learning to new topics.

Work with a partner. What can you learn from these features of animals? Read the example and complete the chart with your ideas.

Animal feature	New product	Applications
Geckos have thousands of tiny hairs on their feet that allow them to climb walls.	A material that has a very strong grip	– Window cleaners can wear special gloves that allow them to climb buildings. – Robot arms on spaceships can use the material to catch loose material in space.
Shark skin is made up of tiny teeth that help to keep the shark clean and allow it to go faster in the water.		
The bill of the toucan bird is incredibly tough, yet it is as light as a plastic cup.		

PREPARE TO LISTEN

A VOCABULARY Listen to the words in bold and discuss their meanings with a partner. Then match the questions (1–10) and the answers (a–j). 🎧 4.3

a. Yes, I do. My role is very **complex**.

b. Yes, it's very **diverse**.

c. Yes, one of my functions is to **fire** people.

d. No, it's my boss's role to **hire** new people.

e. Yes, but he needs to learn **humility**. He needs to learn to be less proud.

f. Yes, she was my **inspiration**.

g. Yes, there's a lot. **Numerous** studies show that it's possible.

h. Yes, I'm going to **reorganize** it.

i. Yes, job **satisfaction** is high.

j. Yes, our **target** is 500 every week.

1. Is there any proof that you can learn to be a leader? _____

2. Does your friend really think he's the best at everything? _____

3. Are there many different kinds of people in your organization? _____

4. Do you have a lot of responsibilities in your job? _____

5. Do you have a number of sales that you have to achieve? _____

6. Do you decide who joins the team? _____

7. Do you decide who loses their job? _____

8. Are the workers in your company happy? _____

9. Are you going to change the way the company is structured? _____

10. Was she the reason you decided to become a manager? _____

B PERSONALIZE Discuss the questions with a partner and explain your answers.

1. Who has been an **inspiration** in your life?

2. Would you want to be the person who **hires** and **fires** people?

3. Do you think **humility** is important in the workplace? In school?

4. Is your community **diverse**?

C Take the leadership quiz. There are no correct answers. Discuss your answers with a partner.

WHAT KIND OF LEADER ARE YOU?

1. The business needs to hire a new person. What should the leader do?
   a. Make the decision alone.
   b. Ask for everyone's opinion and then make the decision.
   c. Let other people make the decision.

2. The sales department needs to be reorganized. What should the leader do?
   a. Just do it and don't ask anyone else.
   b. Ask for everyone's opinions first.
   c. Ask the sales department to do it themselves.

3. The workers are not happy, and job satisfaction is low. What should the leader do?
   a. Nothing—it's not the boss's problem.
   b. Talk to everyone and try to understand the issue.
   c. Help people if they ask for it but not if they don't.

D PERSONALIZE Complete these steps to find your leadership style.

1. Look at your answers to activity B. Are they mostly a, b, or c?
   ▸ If mostly a, you tend to be an **autocratic leader** (one who believes that the leader should make all decisions; doesn't ask workers their opinions).
   ▸ If mostly b, you tend to be **an inclusive leader** (one who believes that the workers should be included in decision making but makes final decisions).
   ▸ If mostly c, you tend to be a **laissez-faire leader** (one who trusts workers completely and allows them to make the decisions).

2. Do you agree with the results of the quiz? Are you that kind of leader?

REFLECT Evaluate leadership styles.

You are going to listen to a talk about successful leadership. What do you think are the advantages and disadvantages of each kind of leadership style? Complete the chart. Then compare your answers with a partner.

Leadership	Advantages	Disadvantages
Autocratic		
Inclusive		
Laissez-faire		

LISTEN & SPEAK
EFFECTIVE **LEADERSHIP SKILLS**

Students and a teacher
at the Prerna Girls
School, Lucknow,
Uttar Pradesh, India

A PREDICT Listen to the beginning of a talk about
leadership. What skills do you think future leaders
will need to have? Discuss with a partner. 🎧 4.4

B PHRASES TO KNOW Match each phrase from the talk to its meaning. Then tell a partner which person you think would be the most difficult to work with.

a. behaves in a way that asks for attention
b. arrives or appears
c. organizes or starts

1. _____ Person 1: He **turns up** to work when he wants. He's often an hour or more late.

2. _____ Person 2: He **sets up** all the meetings, but he never participates or contributes ideas.

3. _____ Person 3: She's always **showing off**. She wants everyone to think she's the best.

NOTE-TAKING TIP

When you are listening to a talk or lecture and have a question, write it down in your notes and highlight it, for example, with a question mark in a circle. That way you can easily find it and ask it at the end of the talk or research the answer later.

⑦ *What skills exactly did leaders need in the past?*

C NOTE TAKING Listen to the talk and take notes. Compare your notes with a partner. Discuss any questions you have. Were your predictions in activity A correct? 🎧 4.5

D MAIN IDEAS Using your notes, check (✓) the three key leadership skills that future leaders need.

1. _____ showing humility
2. _____ making decisions
3. _____ inspiring others
4. _____ trusting others
5. _____ building diverse teams
6. _____ hiring and firing

E MAIN IDEAS Complete the sentences with the correct word or phrase. One is extra.

decisions	diverse teams	humility	inspiration	job satisfaction	motivation	ways of thinking

1. Leaders of the future need to let their workers make more _____.

2. Workers with more control have more _____.

3. Leaders in the future will need to show _____.

4. If the leader shows humility, the workers are likely to have greater _____.

5. Future leaders will need to be able to build _____.

6. Teams where people have different backgrounds have unique _____.

F DETAILS Choose the correct answers. One, two, or all three answers may be correct. Then listen to the talk again and check your answers. 🎧 4.5

1. Semco lets its workers decide how much _____.
   a. they get paid
   b. vacation time they take
   c. profit the company makes

2. Ricardo Semler noticed that the more power and control his workers had, the _____.
   a. more they earned
   b. more they wanted to work
   c. less they did

3. People who inspire us usually _____.
   a. know everything
   b. are perfect
   c. have humility

4. People who have humility usually _____.
   a. make better leaders
   b. make better students
   c. have no chance to improve

5. A leader can only be successful if _____.
   a. they do everything themselves
   b. their team is good
   c. they let the team do everything

6. Compared to teams of similar people, diverse teams tend to _____.
   a. produce better solutions
   b. enjoy their job more
   c. create more profit

G Discuss the questions with a partner.

1. Which of the three skills from the talk do you think is the most important?
2. Which skill do you think you would find easiest/hardest to learn?
3. What other skills do you think business leaders need now or will need in the future?

An online team meeting

You are going to give advice to the owner of a company that is having problems. You will identify some of their leadership challenges and suggest solutions. Use the ideas, vocabulary, and skills from the unit.

H MODEL Listen to advice being given to a business owner. Check (✓) the problem, result, and solution. One, two, or three answers may be correct. 🎧 4.6

Problem 1

a. _____ Employees don't feel respected.

b. _____ Employees feel they are working too hard.

c. _____ Employees spend too much time talking.

Result 1

a. _____ Employees are not working hard.

b. _____ Sales are going down.

c. _____ Profits are going down.

Solution 1

a. _____ Try a more autocratic style of leadership.

b. _____ Allow workers to work from home.

c. _____ Organize an evening out for staff.

Problem 2

a. _____ Customers are unhappy.

b. _____ Customers are not following on social media.

c. _____ Complaints are ignored.

Result 2

a. _____ No one is talking about the company online.

b. _____ There are too many new customers.

c. _____ Customers don't tell their friends to use the company.

Solution 2

a. _____ Hire a new social media manager.

b. _____ Make the team more diverse.

c. _____ Contact customers and ask their opinions.

I With a partner, discuss the problem below, a probable result, and possible solutions.

Problem: The cost of making the product is too high.

GRAMMAR Passive voice with modals

To form the passive with modal and semi-modal verbs (e.g., *could, might, must, should, have to, need to*), use the **modal or semi-modal +** *be* **+ past participle**.

> The relationship with customers **has to be improved**.
> The team **should be given** more responsibilities.

We often use the passive to focus on the person/thing that an action happens to—rather than the person/thing that acts. We also use the passive to be less direct. It allows us to avoid naming the person responsible for an action and is therefore often more polite.

> Active: <u>You should trust employees</u> to do their jobs.
> Passive: **Employees should be trusted** to do their jobs.

J GRAMMAR Rewrite the sentences with passive modals to make them less direct.

1. The boss should trust and respect the staff.

   The staff should be trusted and respected.

2. Management could give employees more control.

   _____

3. Company leadership needs to clearly communicate goals to the team.

   _____

4. The supervisor doesn't have to constantly watch the workers.

   _____

5. The company could increase the number of vacation days.

   _____

6. Management should update the company rules.

   _____

7. The company might offer rewards for success.

   _____

8. The company should share profits with the employees.

   _____

K GRAMMAR Think about a shop or restaurant that you know. Tell a partner five things that could be done to make it better.

The whole restaurant needs to be redecorated. The decor looks old-fashioned.

The menu should be changed, and better ingredients should be used.

PRONUNCIATION   Expressing emotions 🎧4.7

In English, the pitch of your voice (how high or low your voice is) and the intonation of your voice (the movement from high to low or low to high) are very important. The way your voice falls or rises makes the difference in expressing whether you are enthusiastic, neutral, forceful, uncertain, etc. Intonation helps the listener understand your emotion.

Neutral: *It's a great company.*

Enthusiastic: *It's a great company.*

In general, when we want to sound enthusiastic, forceful, or authoritative, we use a higher pitch and more movement in our intonation. Using a lower pitch and a flat intonation often suggests disinterest, or an impersonal attitude.

L PRONUNCIATION Listen and check (✓) the sentences that express enthusiasm or authority. Then repeat those sentences. 🎧4.8

1. a. _____ It's a great company.   b. _____ It's a great company.

2. a. _____ You should be very proud.   b. _____ You should be very proud.

3. a. _____ We've identified a few problems. b. _____ We've identified a few problems.

4. a. _____ We suggest hiring a new person. b. _____ We suggest hiring a new person.

5. a. _____ Your staff should be trusted.   b. _____ Your staff should be trusted.

6. a. _____ The rules need to be changed.   b. _____ The rules need to be changed.

SPEAKING SKILL   Describe trends in graphs and charts

Charts and graphs often show trends. Trends on a graph can refer to quantity (the number) or quality (how good or bad something is). We use the present continuous and certain common phrases to show upward or downward trends.

Quantity	**Quality**

The number of complaints . . .
    is going up.
    is increasing.
    is rising.
	The diversity of the team . . .
	    is improving.
	    is getting better.

Profit . . .
    is going down.
    is decreasing/declining.
    is falling.
	Job satisfaction . . .
	    is getting worse.
	    is decreasing.

M APPLY Work in a small group. Describe the trends in each of the twelve areas.

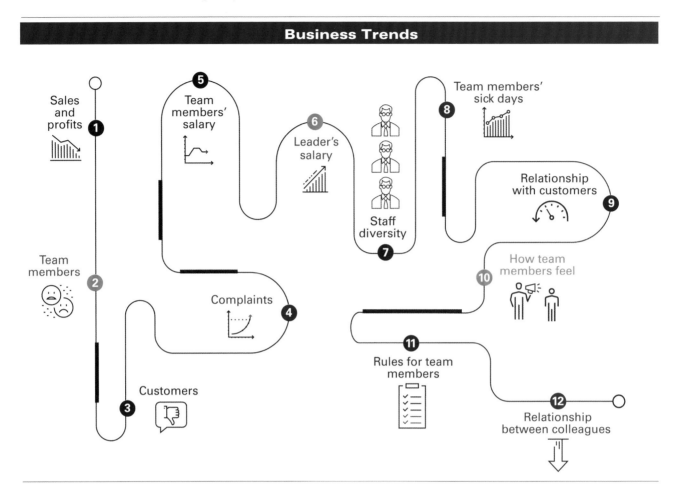

Business Trends

1. Sales and profits
2. Team members
3. Customers
4. Complaints
5. Team members' salary
6. Leader's salary
7. Staff diversity
8. Team members' sick days
9. Relationship with customers
10. How team members feel
11. Rules for team members
12. Relationship between colleagues

N PLAN Choose three trends from activity M and write the numbers in the chart. What problem(s) are causing each trend? What are some solutions? Write your ideas in the chart.

Trends	Problems	Solutions
_____		
_____		
_____		

O PRACTICE With a partner, practice telling a business leader about the company's problems and your solutions. Discuss ways to make your advice clearer and more persuasive.

P UNIT TASK Work in a small group. Present the problems and your advice to the group. Copy the chart above in your notebook, and make notes about the problems and solutions other students talk about. Which person's advice is most similar to yours?

REFLECT

A Check (✓) the Reflect activities you can do and the academic skills you can use.

- ☐ consider how animals lead
- ☐ extend learning to new topics
- ☐ evaluate leadership styles
- ☐ give leadership advice

- ☐ infer meaning
- ☐ describe trends in graphs and charts
- ☐ passive voice with modals
- ☐ extend ideas

B Write the vocabulary words from the unit in the correct column. Add any other words that you learned. Circle words you still need to practice.

NOUN	VERB	ADJECTIVE	ADVERB & OTHER

C Reflect on the ideas in the unit as you answer these questions.

1. What do you remember about leadership in animals?

_____

_____

2. What kind of leader would you like to be?

_____

_____

3. What is the most important thing you learned in this unit?

_____

_____

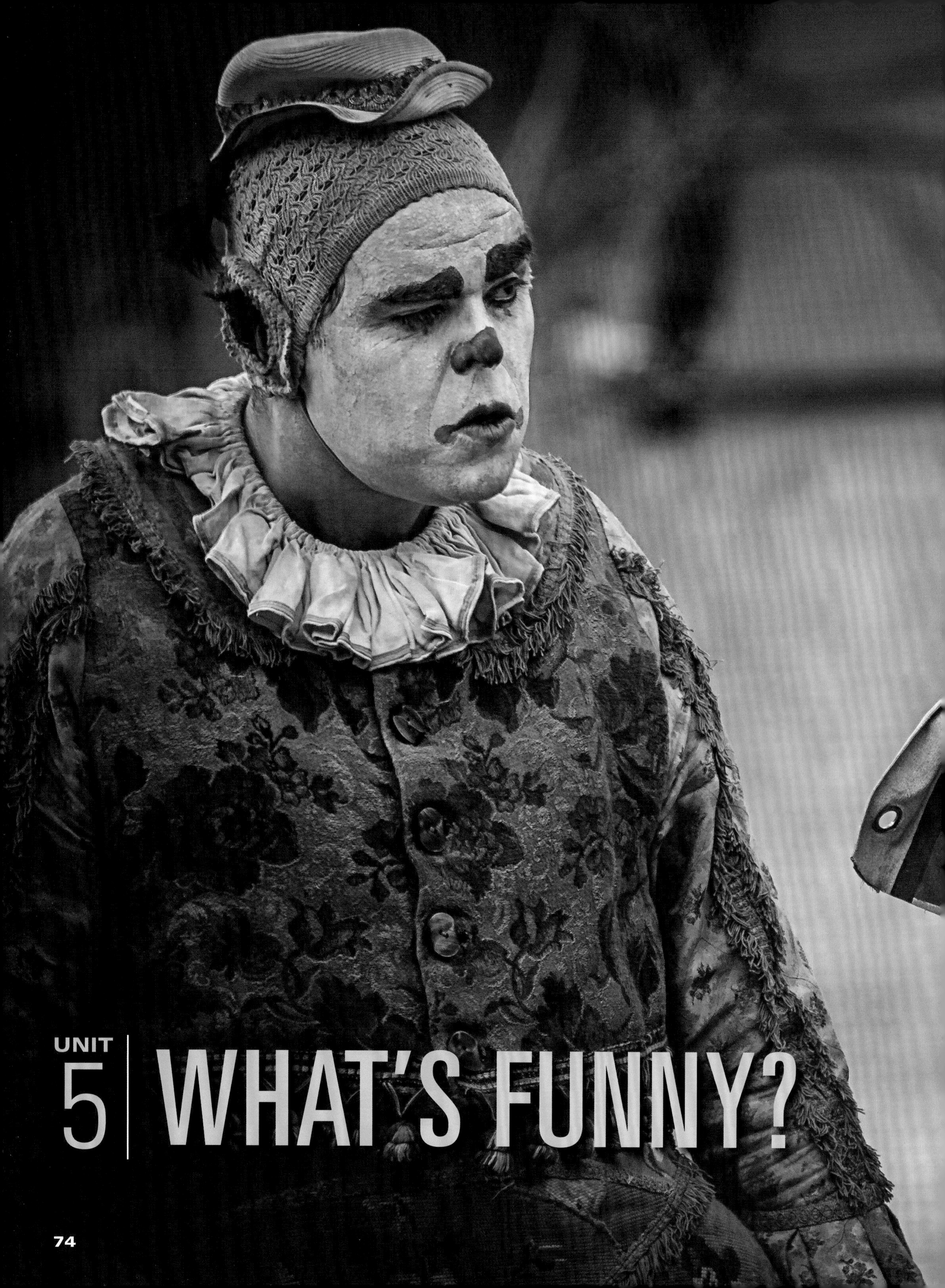

UNIT 5 | WHAT'S FUNNY?

Bucraá Circus
Company, Spain

CONNECT TO THE TOPIC

1. Do you think that clowns like the ones in the photo are funny?

2. In what situations do people try to make other people laugh?

PREPARE TO WATCH

A VOCABULARY Listen to the words and match them with the definitions. Use a dictionary if necessary. ▶ 5.1

1. _____ **comedian** (n)   a. reasonable and understandable

2. _____ **deliberately** (adv)   b. a person whose job is to make people laugh

3. _____ **essentially** (adv)   c. to reduce pain or bad feelings

4. _____ **exaggerated** (adj)   d. basically

5. _____ **humorous** (adj)   e. a person hurt by another person or event

6. _____ **logical** (adj)   f. made bigger and emphasized to make people notice

7. _____ **problematic** (adj)   g. intentionally; on purpose

8. _____ **reality** (n)   h. funny; making you laugh

9. _____ **relieve** (v)   i. the way life really is and not just the way you imagine it

10. _____ **victim** (n)   j. causing difficulties

B VOCABULARY Complete the sentences with the words from activity A.

1. If someone can tell a good joke or a _____ story that makes people laugh, they often find it easier to make friends.

2. Many jokes are _____ because they are hurtful to a person or a group of people. We really need to stop telling these kinds of jokes.

3. A lot of my friends think they can tell funny stories, but the _____ is that only a few of them are good at it and make me laugh.

4. I don't like stories that don't make sense. If a story is not _____, I don't find it interesting.

5. I love puns. _____, they're jokes where the wrong meaning of a word is used. For example, "Did you hear about the guy who lost the *left side* of his body? He's *all right* now."

6. It's never a good idea for an entertainer to explain why a joke is funny. A good _____ never does that, but bad ones sometimes have to.

7. Sometimes, people tell stories about things that happen to them, and the details are _____ and made bigger than life, but that's OK. It makes the story funnier.

8. If you are feeling stressed, watch a funny program on TV or online. It's a great way to _____ stress and make yourself feel better.

9. No one likes being the _____ of a mean joke.

10. Fathers often tell jokes that are not funny. They do it _____, and we even have an expression for these short, not-very-funny jokes: *dad jokes*.

C PERSONALIZE Tell a partner if you agree or disagree with the statements in activity B. Explain your answers.

REFLECT Analyze what makes you laugh.

You are going to watch a video about different kinds of humor. Read the descriptions of four types of comedy shows. Then complete the tasks and share your ideas with a partner.

1. Think of an example for each type of show.
2. Rank the shows from your most favorite (1) to your least favorite (4).

_____ A **sitcom** or **situation comedy** involves a group of characters who deal with funny situations every week. It's not very realistic, but the relationships between the characters are interesting.

_____ A **news comedy** uses stories reported in the mainstream news and adds jokes to summarize the true events. It's often made to look like a real news report.

_____ A **sketch comedy** presents a series of short, humorous scenes, called "sketches." Unlike a sitcom, it does not rely on the same group of characters from week to week.

_____ A **prank reality show** plays tricks on unknowing participants by putting them in strange or absurd situations.

SO, WHAT MAKES YOU LAUGH?

New York,
New York, USA

A MAIN IDEAS Watch the video. Match the types of humor to the descriptions. ▶ 5.1

1. Slapstick humor involves _____
2. Self-deprecating humor involves _____
3. Surreal humor involves _____
4. Practical jokes involve _____
5. Wordplay involves _____

a. events that are not logical.
b. playing tricks on a victim.
c. telling jokes about yourself.
d. humor from words.
e. exaggerated actions.

B DETAILS Watch the video again. Complete the sentences with two or three words. ▶ 5.1

Slapstick

1. An example of slapstick is when somebody gets a cream pie _____.

2. Japanese *kyōgen* involves short performances with _____ _____ action.

Self-deprecating humor

3. The comedian talks about the difference between how he wants to be and how he _____.

4. This humor is _____ in the United States and Canada than many other countries.

Surreal humor

5. This type of humor is more popular in _____ than in the rest of the world.

6. It's a good source of memes because it's _____ in a single image.

Practical jokes

7. They are problematic when they go too far and upset _____.

8. In a practical joke in 1835, a newspaper claimed that there was life _____, including goats and unicorns.

Wordplay

9. In a pun, the _____ of a word is used.

10. All the jokes in the study about favorite jokes were _____.

C PHRASES TO KNOW Complete the excerpt from the video with the phrases. Then discuss the differences in meaning with a partner.

laugh about	laughing at	laughing with

When the victim feels that people are ¹_____ them and not
²_____ them, and when the victim can also
³_____ the joke afterward, then it's a successful practical joke.

D In a small group, read the three jokes aloud. Help each other to understand the jokes. Then discuss what style of humor each one is and whether you find it funny.

1. A: Why was six afraid of seven?

    B: Because seven ate nine.

2. A: Can I have a coffee without milk?

    B: Sorry, we don't have any milk, but you can have it without cream.

3. A: Have you ever felt like your entire life is just a big school exam?
    B: Yes, and I'm quite certain that I forgot to study for it.

GRAMMAR   Comparative forms

We use different forms to talk about similarities and differences.

Adjectives

To show that two things are different, add -er (+ *than*) to one-syllable and some two-syllable adjectives. With longer adjectives, use *more/less* + adjective (+ *than*).

> *Surreal humor is much **stranger than** other types of humor.*
> *It's **less popular** in some countries (**than** in others).*

To show that two things are (not) the same, use (*not*) *as* + adjective + *as*.

> *In my country, surreal humor is **as popular as** slapstick humor.*

Adverbs

Adverbs follow the same rules as adjectives.

> *That comedian speaks **faster than** the others.*
> *Memes are **more easily** shared than other kinds of humor.*
> *I **don't** like slapstick **as much as** other kinds of humor.*

Nouns

With nouns, use *more* + noun + *than*.

> *She knows **more jokes than** I do.*

Use (*not*) *as many / much* + noun + *as*.

> *I **don't** know **as many jokes as** my friend does.*
> *We have **as much time as** we did last week.*

E GRAMMAR Complete the sentences with a comparative form.

1. Her jokes are very funny. Mine are not very funny.

   Her jokes are _____ mine.

2. My story was very humorous. Hers was very humorous, too.

   My story was _____ hers.

3. My friend, Tan, cries very easily at films. My friend, Sonia, doesn't cry very easily at films.

   Tan cries _____ at films than Sonia.

4. I smile a little bit. I used to smile a lot.

   I don't smile _____ I used to.

5. I've seen several comedies recently. He hasn't seen any comedies this year.

   I've seen _____ he has.

F GRAMMAR Underline the comparative forms in these sentences. Then take turns asking and answering the questions with a partner.

1. Do you have more homework now than you did a year ago?
2. Do you have more friends now than you had five years ago?
3. Do you buy more clothes than you used to?
4. Are you more independent than you were a year ago?
5. Do you laugh as much as you did when you were younger?
6. Can you understand English better than you did a year ago?

REFLECT   Consider the role of humor in your life.

Read the statements and check (✓) your response. Then work with a partner. Explain and compare your responses. How are you the same? How are you different?

	No, not at all.	Sometimes.	Yes, absolutely.
1. I find it easy to remember jokes.			
2. I find it difficult to tell jokes.			
3. I laugh a lot when I'm alone.			
4. I enjoy watching romantic comedies.			
5. I find slapstick humor very funny.			
6. People find me naturally funny.			

PREPARE TO LISTEN

A VOCABULARY Listen to the words in bold and choose the correct meaning. 🎧 5.2

1. I don't think these two paragraphs **belong** together. They're not even about the same topic.

   a. fit or go   b. exist   c. join or attach

2. I don't have high **expectations** for the comedy show tonight. The tickets were cheap and none of the comedians are well known.

   a. what one hopes will happen   b. what one thinks will happen   c. what one knows will happen

3. He looks mean and unfriendly, but he's **harmless**.

   a. honest   b. not dangerous   c. not friendly

4. I don't like humor that's mean and suggests that some people are **inferior** to others.

   a. not as good as   b. better than   c. the same as

5. You should look at the situation from her **perspective** before you reach a conclusion.

   a. opinion   b. position   c. background

6. It was a **relief** when I finally passed my exams. I felt I could relax again.

   a. feeling of ease   b. feeling of unhappiness   c. feeling of boredom

7. The things that happened in the film were **ridiculous** and would never happen in real life, but it was funny anyway.

   a. very clever   b. very silly   c. very normal

8. She uses humor to suggest that she's smarter, more talented, and, to put it simply, just **superior** to everyone else.

   a. not as good as   b. better than   c. the same as

9. The last time they met they had a big argument, so when they saw each other this time, there was **tension** in the room.

   a. unhappiness   b. sadness   c. nervousness

10. I don't like him. I think his behavior is **threatening**, and I don't know what he will do next.

    a. making you feel tired   b. making you feel relaxed   c. making you feel danger

B PERSONALIZATION Discuss these questions with a partner.

1. What kind of **expectations** should we have for our friends?

2. Do you find films from your country **superior** or **inferior** to Hollywood films?

3. What kind of humor do you find **harmless**? What kind can cause **tension**?

4. What's the most **ridiculous** thing you have ever seen or done?

"That book is not available at this branch, this
library system or this solar system,
but we can order it for you."

Here are different ways to respond to jokes in English.

😃 *That's a good one!/Very funny!*

🙁 *Hmm . . . maybe that's not my kind of humor.*

😕 *I don't get it! Can you explain?*

C APPLY Listen to three jokes and check (✓) your response. Compare your
response with a partner. Use a phrase from the Communication Tip. 🎧 5.3

	I think it's funny.	I don't think it's funny.	I don't understand it.
Joke 1			
Joke 2			
Joke 3			

REFLECT   Tell a joke.

You are going to listen to a talk on different theories of why jokes are funny.
Work with a partner and tell your favorite joke or a joke that you have heard
before. Note your partner's reaction to your joke. Then discuss why you
think each joke is funny or not.

LISTEN & SPEAK

WHY IS THAT FUNNY?
FOUR THEORIES ABOUT HUMOR

A PREVIEW Listen to the introduction to a talk. The introduction contains a joke. Try to remember it and retell it to a partner. 🎧 **5.4**

B MAIN IDEAS Listen to the talk and match the theories to the explanations. 🎧 **5.5**

1. _____ Superiority theory

2. _____ Incongruity theory

3. _____ Relief theory

4. _____ Benign challenge theory

a. We laugh because someone breaks a rule or norm but in a safe way.

b. We laugh because an object or an action is strange or unexpected in that situation.

c. We laugh because it makes us feel that we are better or smarter than the person in the joke.

d. We laugh because, at first, we feel stressed, but then everything turns out OK and we feel better.

C PHRASES TO KNOW Read the definitions.
Complete the sentences with the correct form of the phrases.

out of place: wrong in that situation
pull out: to take something out of another thing
walk into: to hit something accidentally when you aren't looking

1. The first hunter quickly _____ his mobile phone.

2. Take the person who isn't looking and _____ a streetlight.

3. Something which is incongruous is _____.

D DETAILS Listen to the four theories again. Then answer each question. 🎧 5.5

Superiority theory

1. According to this theory, why do we laugh when someone walks into a streetlight?

   _____

2. What types of humor can this theory *not* explain?

   _____

Incongruity theory

3. According to the speaker, where would a boat be incongruous?

   _____

4. What, in short, is the problem with this theory?

   _____

Relief theory

5. According to this theory, what happens to the tension that we feel in a joke?

   _____

6. What kind of humor can this theory *not* explain?

   _____

Benign challenge theory

7. What does *benign* mean?

   _____

8. According to this theory, what is challenged in wordplay?

   _____

Western Cape Province,
South Africa

LISTENING SKILL Recognize connectors in speech

Recognizing **connectors** in speech can help you understand what a speaker has said and what they are going to say. Here are some common connectors.

▸ To add similar information: **moreover**, **furthermore**, **in addition**

   Moreover, *superiority theory explains why everyone hates being laughed at.*

▸ To add similar information that is less important: **incidentally**, **by the way**

   This, ***incidentally***, *happened in an art museum in the Netherlands.*

▸ To introduce contrasting information: **the problem/trouble is that . . .** , **on the other hand**

   The problem *with this theory* ***is that*** *it can't explain surreal humor.*

▸ To restate information: **to put it another way**, **put simply**

   To put it another way, *it's incongruous and therefore funny.*

▸ To summarize information: **in short**, **to summarize**

   In short, *incongruity theory just seems too simple.*

E APPLY Listen to the section on incongruity theory again. Number these connectors in the order that you hear them. 🎧 5.6

a. _____ in short

b. _____ moreover

c. _____ incidentally

d. _____ to put it another way

e. _____ the trouble is that . . .

F APPLY Listen and check (✓) the sentence that naturally follows what the speaker says. 🎧 5.7

1. a. _____ . . . my grandfather was a comedian, too.

    b. _____ . . . my grandfather was a police officer.

2. a. _____ . . . they don't always realize that they are doing this.

    b. _____ . . . they try to make other people feel inferior.

3. a. _____ . . . it doesn't explain why we don't laugh at serious accidents.

    b. _____ . . . it also explains why we laugh at self-deprecating humor.

4. a. _____ . . . the joke was a big success.

    b. _____ . . . some people called to ask where they could buy a spaghetti tree.

Los Angeles,
California, USA

Give a presentation about humor in your country.

You are going to present a profile of humor in your country in general and for your generation in particular. You will talk about the importance of humor, how people watch and enjoy it, and what kind of humor they prefer. Use the ideas, vocabulary, and skills from the unit.

G MODEL Listen to a student. Take notes and then use your notes to complete the chart. 🎧 5.8

	My country in general	My generation
1. How important is humor?	☐ very important ☐ fairly important ☐ not very important	☐ very important ☐ fairly important ☐ not very important
2. Where do people look to find humor?	☐ on TV ☐ in books ☐ on mobile phones	☐ on TV ☐ in books ☐ on mobile phones
3. What are the most popular types of humor?	☐ slapstick ☐ practical jokes ☐ surreal humor	☐ slapstick ☐ practical jokes ☐ surreal humor

H Listen again and check your answers in activity G. 🎧 5.8

SPEAKING SKILL   Introduce contrasting information

There are various ways to point out differences between ideas when speaking.

Contrast an idea in a previous sentence

In general, people like to watch humorous shows on TV. **In contrast**, *my generation uses their mobile phones to watch comedy.*

My friends and I often share short, funny videos. The older generation, **on the other hand**, *doesn't seem to share as many things online.*

We often tell funny stories. **However**, *we rarely tell jokes.*

Contrast ideas between two clauses

He thought the joke was funny, **but** *no one laughed.*

We're constantly watching humorous things **although** *we don't often watch them on TV.*

While *most people like slapstick, my generation prefers practical jokes.*

The average person likes slapstick, **whereas** *we prefer surreal memes.*

I   APPLY Use the chart to compare different generations with a partner. Change any details in the table that you think are not correct.

Most baby boomers prefer to use telephones to communicate, whereas millennials prefer to use instant messages.

	Baby boomers	Generation X	Millennials	Generation Z
	between 1946 and 1964	between 1965 and 1979	between 1980 and late 90s	between the late 90s and 2010s
Preferred way to communicate	telephone	email	instant message	emoji
Global population when they were born	3 billion	4 billion	5.5 billion	7.5 billion
Significant development or innovation for this generation	moon landings	first personal computers	beginning of social media	rise of algorithms and A.I.

CRITICAL THINKING   Avoid stereotypes

A **stereotype** is a fixed, often negative idea about a group of people. Stereotypes lead us to believe that all people in a group are the same when, in fact, people within a group are different. Stereotypes have a negative impact on us because they prevent us from seeing people, groups, and society clearly and fairly. They interfere with our ability to think critically.

J APPLY Work with a small group. What stereotypes do people make about your generation? Do you agree with any of the stereotypes? Explain.

PRONUNCIATION   Focus words in contrasting information 🎧5.9

Important content words (nouns, verbs, adjectives, etc.) are usually stressed, but when the speaker contrasts information, the words that contain the contrast will have extra stress.

> *Baby boomers watch funny shows on TV, but **my** generation likes to watch funny things on their **mobile phones**.*

> *We like stories, but telling jokes is **not** something we do very much.*

K PRONUNCIATION Listen and underline the words with the contrasting information. Then listen again and repeat. 🎧5.10

1. She likes slapstick, but I prefer self-deprecating humor.
2. We watch humor online, but they usually watch it on TV.
3. In contrast to my peers, I don't enjoy practical jokes.
4. The average person likes slapstick, whereas we prefer surreal memes.

L PRONUNCIATION Read the sentences and underline the words that you expect to be the contrasting information. Then listen, check your answers, and repeat. 🎧5.11

1. Generation Z was born between the late 90s and 2010s, while Generation X was born much earlier.
2. I'm a fan of surreal humor although my parents hate it.
3. In contrast to my friends, I don't spend hours online watching videos.
4. I felt relaxed, while some people felt there was a lot of tension in the room.
5. Everybody loves humor; however, not everyone loves the same kind of humor.
6. I like watching funny videos, but it might be more fun making them.

M PLAN Make notes in the chart to answer the questions.

	My country in general	My generation
How important is humor?		
Where do people look to find humor (e.g., TV, magazines, online, etc.)?		
What are the most popular types of humor?		

N PRACTICE Use your notes and this checklist to practice your presentation.

Have you included . . . ?

☐ a contrast between your country in general and your generation

☐ examples from you and your friends

☐ phrases to introduce contrasting information

☐ a summary of the information in your talk

☐ vocabulary from this unit

O UNIT TASK Work in groups of three or four and present your information. As you listen to other students, take notes. Which person's ideas are most similar to yours?

The Westcar Papyrus (c. 1600 BC) is an Egyptian text that contains an example of one of the earliest jokes.

REFLECT

A Check (✓) the Reflect activities you can do and the academic skills you can use.

☐ analyze what makes you laugh

☐ consider the role of humor in your life

☐ tell a joke

☐ give a presentation about humor in your country

☐ recognize connectors in speech

☐ introduce contrasting information

☐ comparative forms

☐ avoid stereotypes

B Write the vocabulary words from the unit in the correct column. Add any other words that you learned. Circle words you still need to practice.

NOUN	VERB	ADJECTIVE	ADVERB & OTHER

C Reflect on the ideas in the unit as you answer these questions.

1. What was the most interesting thing that you learned about humor?

_____

_____

2. How can a good sense of humor help you in life?

_____

_____

3. What is the most important thing you learned in this unit?

_____

_____

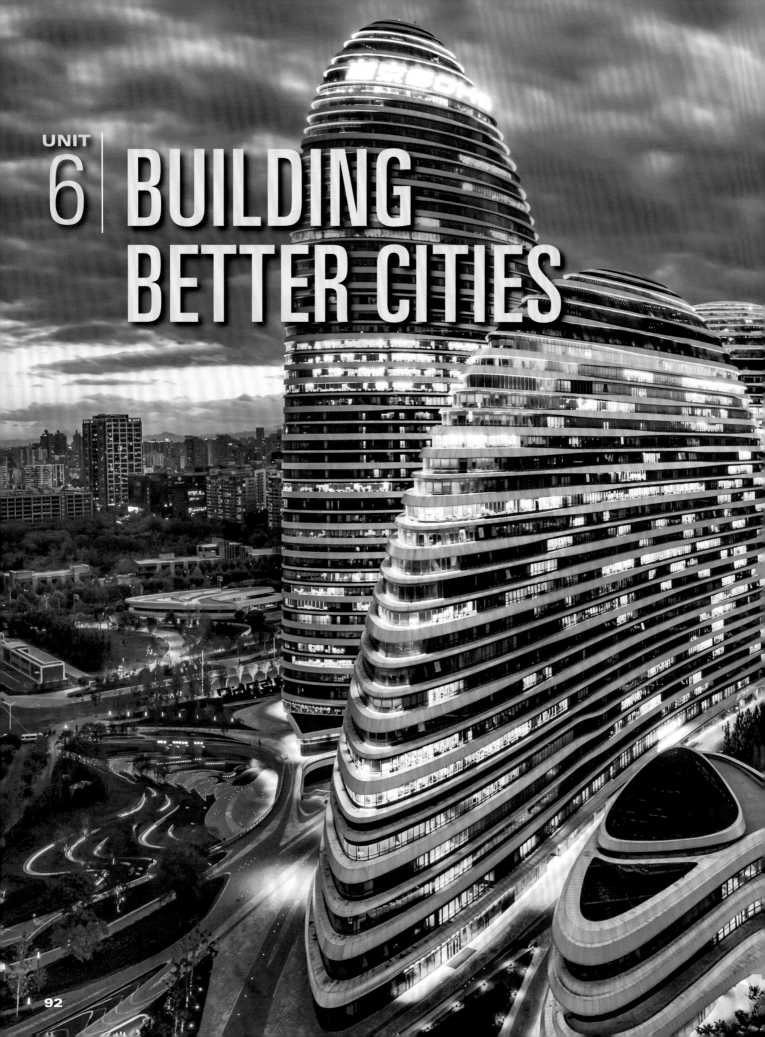

Wangjing SOHO is a complex of three skyscrapers in Beijing, China.

CONNECT TO THE TOPIC

1. Look at the photo. What do you think of this building? Do you like it or not?

2. In what ways has your city changed since you first knew it?

93

PREPARE TO LISTEN

A VOCABULARY Listen to the words and read the definitions. Complete the sentences with the correct form of the words. 🔊 6.1

---

argue (v) to give an opinion or reasons for an opinion
authority (n) people with official responsibility for something (e.g., the local health authority)
compact (adj) closely arranged together and using little space
demolish (v) to destroy
factor (n) a reason for something
ideal (adj) perfect; the best that something can be
layout (n) the way that a place is arranged
principle (n) an idea that explains how something happens or works
propose (v) to suggest
urban (adj) relating to a town or city

---

1. Almost 60 percent of the world's population lives in _____ areas. The rest live in smaller towns or the countryside.

2. There are many different reasons that people move from the countryside to the city, but one important _____ is employment opportunities.

3. The city is building a new sports stadium even though citizens _____ against spending money on one.

4. The _____ city is safe, inexpensive, and convenient. It's also close to nature so that people can enjoy the outdoors easily. There are not many cities like this.

5. Cities that are spread out over a wide area are much less sustainable than cities that are _____, where people can drive less and use public transportation more.

6. Old buildings are often _____ to make way for new ones.

7. In the 1970s, in the Dutch city of Utrecht, the local _____ decided to build a 12-lane freeway over part of the 900-year-old canal around the city. It was completed in 1978.

8. In the 1990s, the city of Utrecht _____ changing the freeway back into a canal. The local people agreed, and the work began. It took 20 years and was completed in 2020.

9. Urban planners are responsible for the _____ of a city. They make decisions about what can be built and how different parts of a city can be used.

10. The basic _____ of public transportation is to help people travel around a city as quickly and easily as possible, without a car.

Picture A

Picture B

B In your opinion, which picture does each sentence describe better? Check (✓) the picture. Then compare your answers with a partner and explain your choices.

	Picture A	Picture B
1. The **layout** of the area is interesting and attractive.	_____	_____
2. The main **principle** is to use the space efficiently.	_____	_____
3. It's a very **compact** place.	_____	_____
4. It's hard to **demolish** buildings here.	_____	_____
5. One **factor** that brings people here is the desire for community.	_____	_____
6. Many people would think this is an **ideal** place to raise a family.	_____	_____

REFLECT   Evaluate the pros and cons of living environments.

You are going to listen to a podcast about urban planning—how to design cities and city spaces. Discuss these questions with a partner.

1. What are the similarities and differences between the two places shown in activity B?
2. What are the pros and cons of living in each type of environment?
3. In which environment would you rather live? Explain.

HOW TO PLAN A CITY

A MAIN IDEAS Listen to the podcast. Choose the correct answers. 🎧 6.2

1. What is the topic of this podcast?

   a. How to improve our existing urban spaces

   b. How to build better cities

   c. Both of the above

2. What does the urban planner believe about cities?

   a. Bigger is better.

   b. Cities shouldn't be too big.

   c. Size is not important.

3. What does the architect believe?

   a. The old parts of a city shouldn't be demolished.

   b. You improve a city by demolishing the older areas.

   c. A city is better when it doesn't change.

4. What else does the architect believe about the buildings in a city?

   a. They should be similar to each other.

   b. There should be a different place for each kind of building.

   c. There should be different kinds of buildings in the same area.

Hội An, Quảng Nam Province, Vietnam

B DETAILS Listen again. Complete the sentences with two or three words. 🎧6.2

1. The first principle for the city planner is that cities should _____ and easy to travel around.

2. Bigger cities are often _____ because they need more highways.

3. The urban planner's role is to make travel times in a city no more than
    _____.

4. One hundred and twenty _____ are being built around the world at the moment.

5. If a public square is more than 100 feet across, it becomes difficult to recognize
    _____.

6. The architect argues that once you _____, you can't change your mind.

7. Le Corbusier wanted to demolish parts of the city center of Paris and replace them with
    _____.

8. The parts of Paris that Le Corbusier wanted to knock down had problems with
    _____.

9. Jane Jacobs believed that when a city has a mix of buildings, it brings
    _____.

C PHRASES TO KNOW Match the phrases in bold from the listening to the correct meanings. Then discuss with a partner whether you agree with each statement.

a. to demand	b. to demolish	c. to note or comment

1. _____ A lot of people are now **calling for** cars to be banned from city centers.

2. _____ Many people have **pointed out** that old cities are not always more beautiful than new ones.

3. _____ We shouldn't **knock down** any building that is more than 100 years old.

D Read the excerpts from the listening. Discuss the questions with a partner.

1. "Historian Lewis Mumford claimed that the city was the second most important invention ever." Do you agree? If not, what do you think the most important invention was?

2. "Peter Calthorpe estimates that over the next 30 years we'll have to find urban space for another 3 billion people." How do you think we will do this? What are the dangers of doing or not doing this?

Artist's drawing of a future city

LISTENING SKILL   Understand reporting verbs

Speakers use a variety of **reporting verbs** to introduce other people's ideas. It's important to recognize when a speaker is doing this rather than giving their own ideas.

*Experts **report** that cities are growing faster than ever before.*

Reporting verbs are used for different purposes:

▸ To report a fact or observation: *explain, mention, observe, point out, report*
▸ To report an opinion: *agree, believe, claim, estimate*
▸ To report advice: *advise, argue, propose, recommend, suggest*
▸ To report a request for action: *call for, demand, encourage*

E   APPLY Listen and complete the paragraph with reporting verbs. 🔊6.3

Some urban planners ¹_____ that our country will need another 20 new cities

in the next decade. That's an ambitious goal. Many planners are ²_____ that all new

cities should be 30-minute cities, that is cities that allow you to travel anywhere in 30 minutes without

a car. They are also ³_____ these new cities to be smart and environmentally

friendly. Some other urban planners have ⁴_____ that this estimate may be too low,

and we may need more than 20 new cities. Whatever the number, everyone ⁵_____

that we start building now.

F   APPLY Choose the speaker's purpose for using each reporting verb in activity E.

1. a. To report an opinion   b. To report a request for action

2. a. To report a fact or observation   b. To report advice

3. a. To report an opinion   b. To report a request for action

4. a. To report a fact or observation   b. To report advice

5. a. To report advice   b. To report a request for action

CRITICAL THINKING   Identify criteria and constraints

When thinking about solutions to problems, it helps to identify the criteria and the constraints before you reach a solution. The **criteria** are what must be achieved for the solution to be successful. The **constraints** are the limitations that make it harder to find a solution. For example, imagine you want to move to a new city.

PROBLEM	CRITERIA	CONSTRAINTS
What city should I move to?	I want it to be small, beautiful and close to nature.	Houses must be cheap to rent.

SOLUTION

G APPLY Listen and take notes. Then complete the chart. 🎧 6.4

Problem	How to build a ¹_____ in Milan
Criteria for success	The building had to be ²_____. It also had to be ³_____.
Constraints	The budget: € ⁴_____ The weather: It's ⁵_____.
Solution	Two apartment buildings covered in ⁶_____

REFLECT   Propose a solution to an urban problem.

Work with a small group and read the information. Find a solution to the problem that takes account of the criteria for success and the constraints.

Problem	Your town has an empty building near the center. The building is an old hall, about 150 feet long by 50 feet wide (45 meters by 15 meters). The city authorities want to find a new use for the building.
Criteria for success	It should create jobs. It should be a space that everyone can enjoy. It has to make money for the city.
Constraints	The space can't be used for shops or restaurants. The budget is only $500,000. The building should open as soon as possible.
Solution	

PREPARE TO WATCH

A VOCABULARY Listen to the words. Read the sentences and write the words that can replace the underlined phrases. Use a dictionary if necessary. 🎧 6.5

cluster (n)	feature (n)	maintenance (n)	revenue (n)	sustainability (n)
economic (adj)	filter (v)	portion (n)	sensible (adj)	system (n)

1. In swimming pools, special devices are used to <u>remove dirt from</u> the water. That means that you don't need to change the water very often. _____

2. It's <u>practical</u> to have a good public transportation system in a city. It helps people travel around quickly and cheaply. _____

3. A lot of young adults that I know live at home with their parents. If they don't, they have to use a <u>part</u> of their income on rent. That can be expensive. _____

4. We have two separate containers for things we throw away. One is for recyclables. The other is for non-recyclables. It's a good <u>way of organizing things</u>. _____

5. Some cities use <u>the money that they make</u> from parking fees to improve the roads.
   _____

6. In my town, there's a <u>small group</u> of factories <u>close together</u>, and the hot water that the factories produce is used to heat our houses. It's a great idea. _____

7. In my opinion, all modern homes should have solar panels. They're a <u>characteristic</u> of environmentally friendly houses. _____

8. People generally move to my town for <u>money and finance-related</u> reasons. It's easy to find work, and the cost of living is not too high. _____

9. <u>Keeping something alive and not damaging it</u> is not only an environmental necessity. It's also important for society and the economy. _____

10. I don't want to have a car or a garden. They both need a lot of <u>work to keep them in good condition</u>. _____

B PERSONALIZE Discuss these questions with a partner.

1. What **features** make a city a good place to live?

2. What's an example of something you've done that was not **sensible**?

3. Do you have a good **system** for learning new vocabulary? Explain.

C Listen to four conversations. Then complete the infographic. 🎧 6.6

Sustainable Initiatives

**Cities cover 3% of the Earth's land but produce 60% of greenhouse gases.
Which cities are tackling this problem?**

Bogotá, Colombia

has ^{1}_____ kilometers of bike lanes and plans to add 280 more.

Pontevedra, Spain

has ^{2}_____ cars in the city center.

Singapore

demands that any plants and trees removed on the ground be replaced with plants and trees in the sky (on buildings).

Freiburg, Germany

demands that all new houses are low energy.

San Francisco, USA

has cut water usage to ^{3}_____ gallons per person per day. (The average is 80-100 gallons.)

Vancouver, Canada

has banned ^{4}_____ plastics.

REFLECT   Consider initiatives for improving urban sustainability.

Before you watch a video about a sustainable city, discuss these questions with a partner.

1. Look at the six initiatives in activity C. What problems is each initiative trying to solve?

2. Which one do you think is most likely to make a significant difference? Explain.

3. Choose one initiative and make a list of criteria for success and constraints.

THE SUSTAINABLE CITY

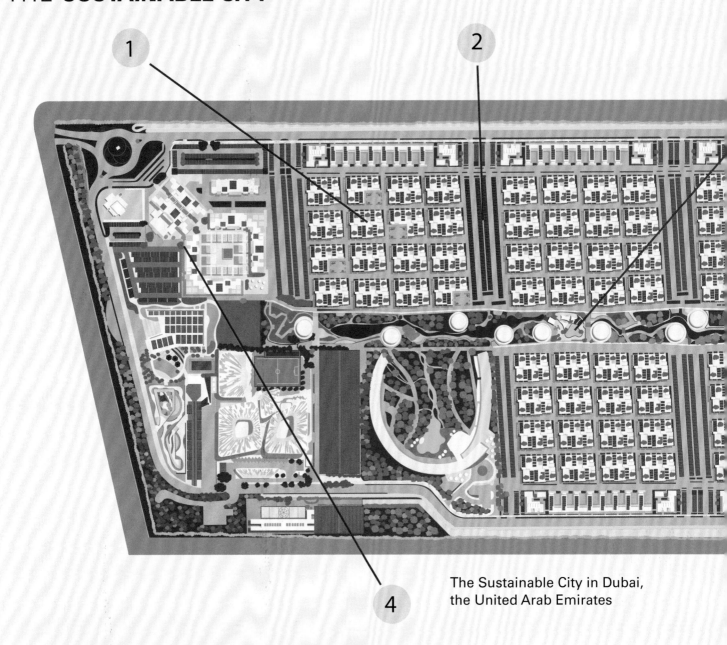

The Sustainable City in Dubai, the United Arab Emirates

A PREDICT Look at the map. What do you think the different parts of the city are for? Match a number from the map to a part of the city.

a. _____ An area that is open to the public

b. _____ Car parking space covered with solar panels

c. _____ A cluster of villas (or homes) where people live

d. _____ A community swimming pool for all residents

B MAIN IDEAS Watch the video. Write T for *True* or F for *False*. Then correct the false statements. ▶ 6.1

1. _____ The villas are kept naturally cool.

2. _____ They don't allow cars in the city.

3. _____ They use wind to create their own electricity.

4. _____ They have an environmentally friendly pool.

5. _____ Residents pay high maintenance fees.

C DETAILS Choose the correct answers. Then watch the video again and check your answers. ▶ 6.1

1. Each villa faces **north / south / east** to benefit from the shade and stay cooler.

2. The cars are kept away from the **swimming pool / car parks / villas**.

3. They have **hundreds / thousands / millions** of solar panels in the Sustainable City.

4. The swimming pool has a **closed / open / heated**, filtered system.

5. At the moment, the weather is **25 / 35 / 45** degrees Celsius.

6. At the entrance to the city, there are buildings that people can **design / purchase / rent**.

7. Services, such as cleaning the streets and the solar panels, are **free / cheap / expensive** for residents.

D PHRASES TO KNOW Read the statements from the video. Choose the correct meaning for the phrases in bold.

1. We avoid the sun, and that is so important. Otherwise, air conditioning cost is going to **go through the roof**.

   a. increase a lot   b. increase a little bit

2. We wanted to keep the cars away from the clusters of homes. Every cluster is completely **car free**.

   a. Cars don't have to pay.   b. There are no cars.

3. For our solar power, we have 10-megawatt peak installed. To **put** that **into perspective**, that's the same as 40,000 solar panels.

   a. explain the reasons why   b. compare with something familiar

E Discuss the questions in a small group.

1. What are the most impressive features of the Sustainable City?

2. Would you like to live in a city like this? Explain.

3. Do you know of any other cities like this?

PRONUNCIATION   Linking words 🎧6.7

When we speak, we sometimes add a sound to link two words. We do this when the first word ends in a vowel sound and the second word begins with one. The extra sound makes the two words flow together more naturally.

When a word ends in the vowel sounds /i^y/ or /ay/ and the next word begins with a vowel sound, the two sounds are usually linked together with a /y/ sound.

we /y/ are   why /y/ is

When a word ends in the vowel sounds /o^w/ or /u^w/ and the next word begins with a vowel sound, the two sounds are usually linked together with a /w/ sound.

so /w/ if   who /w/ are

F PRONUNCIATION Write the sound, /y/ or /w/, that joins each pair of words. Listen, check your answers, and repeat the words. 🎧6.8

1. zero /_____/ energy

2. very /_____/ old

3. try /_____/ again

4. to /_____/ ask

5. buy /_____/ it

6. she /_____/ asked

7. no /_____/ idea

8. may /_____/ I

9. go /_____/ away

G PRONUNCIATION Read the sentences. Write the two words that link together and add the /y/ or a /w/. Then listen, check, and repeat. 🎧6.9

1. This is a series about energy of the future.

   _____energy_____ /__y__/ _____of_____

2. They get a lot of shade, and we avoid the sun.

   _____ /_____/ _____

3. That is so important in this part of the world.

   _____ /_____/ _____

4. We decided to orient them all toward the north.

   _____ /_____/ _____

5. We actually have 10 megawatts installed.

   _____ /_____/ _____

6. It's going to go up a lot.

   _____ /_____/ _____

Please be Seated by Paul Cocksedge, London, UK

UNIT TASK   Present a plan for a new public space.

You are going to present your ideas for an initiative to improve a particular area of your town or community. Think about the purpose of your initiative and how it will make your town or community a better place to live. You might also think about the sustainability of the initiative. Use the ideas, vocabulary, and skills from the unit.

H MODEL Listen to a student proposing a new initiative for her town. Answer the questions. 🎧6.10

1.   Which building is the student proposing to knock down? _____

2.   What is the student proposing to replace it with? _____

I   Listen again and complete the details for the new public space. 🎧6.10

Problem it solves	
Special features	
Criteria for success	
Constraints on success	

J RESEARCH Before the next lesson, do the following short survey. Ask some people who live in your town or community the following two questions. Note their answers.

1.   Is there a building in this town that should be demolished? What should replace it?

2.   What other changes to a building or area would improve the town?

GRAMMAR Reporting verbs

Reporting verbs are used to talk about what someone has said or written. They can also give information about the speaker's attitude and intention. Notice the difference in attitude:

Neutral attitude: *He **said** that the library should be torn down.*
Strong attitude: *He **argued** that the library should be torn down.*

The most common patterns for these verbs are:

▸ **Verb + *that***: *argue, believe, claim, estimate, explain, hope, point out, propose, recommend, report, suggest, say, state*

*Zaha Hadid **claimed that** architecture is about helping people to feel good.*

▸ **Verb + object + *that***: *advise, convince, persuade*

*Most experts **advised the city authorities that** they should demolish the building.*

Some of these verbs can also be used in other patterns:

▸ **Verb + -*ing***: *propose, recommend, suggest*

*Some people **suggested building** a new shopping center.*

▸ **Verb + object + infinitive**: *advise, convince, persuade*

*Most experts **advised the city authorities to demolish** the building.*

K GRAMMAR Choose the correct words. In three sentences, both choices are possible.

1. Most people argued **that / me that** it should be demolished.

2. One person tried to persuade me **that I should / to** move to a modern building.

3. Philip Johnson claimed **that / me that** the job of an architect is to create beautiful buildings.

4. Antoni Gaudi advised other architects **to follow / following** nature in their designs.

5. Several people who I talked to proposed **that we demolish / demolishing** the new bus station.

6. One person pointed out **that it was / us that it was** quite a new building.

7. Ten people suggested **that I should talk / talking** to the local authority about my ideas.

8. My uncle convinced **that / me that** architecture was a good subject to study.

L GRAMMAR Complete these sentences with your own ideas. Then share your sentences with a partner.

1. Someone once advised me _____.

2. I have a friend who argues that _____.

3. My family persuaded me _____.

4. My parents recommended _____.

SPEAKING SKILL   Present persuasively

When you present your ideas to an audience, you want them to consider the ideas carefully and possibly take action. This means that you need to be persuasive. Use these techniques to make your presentations more persuasive.

1. Support your opinions and ideas with the words of experts.
   The **famous architect Zaha Hadid** claimed that . . .

2. Refer to people in general to support your opinions and ideas.
   Many people claim that they feel lost in a public square that is too big.

3. Use forceful words like *strongly*, *urgently*, and *definitely* to talk about what you believe.
   I **strongly** believe that great design should be ambitious.

4. Repeat important words and phrases to emphasize your point. Use parallel forms to do this.
   This new public space **will appeal** to adults, it **will appeal** to teenagers, and it **will appeal** to children.

M APPLY In your notebook, write new sentences to make these statements more persuasive.

1. I would like to have more public space in our town.
2. Great towns need a mix of buildings.
3. I think that a new public square will really benefit our town.
4. In the next 30 years, we will need city space for 3 billion more people.

Designers presenting their plans

N PLAN Work with a partner. Explain the results of your research from activity J. Then use the chart to plan your presentation together. Make a drawing of your proposal if possible.

Demolish a building? What?	
Build what?	
Problem it solves	
Special features	
Criteria for success	
Constraints	

O PRACTICE Work with your partner and practice giving your presentation. Discuss with your partner how to make your presentation more persuasive.

P UNIT TASK Work in groups and give your presentation. Copy the chart in activity N into your notebook and take notes as you listen to the other pairs in your group. Which proposal will be the most successful in making your town a better place to live?

Paprocany Lake Shore, Tychy, Poland

REFLECT

A Check (✓) the Reflect activities you can do and the academic skills you can use.

- ☐ evaluate pros and cons of living environments
- ☐ propose a solution to an urban problem
- ☐ consider initiatives for improving urban sustainability
- ☐ present a plan for a new public space

- ☐ understand reporting verbs
- ☐ present persuasively
- ☐ reporting verbs
- ☐ identify criteria and constraints

B Write the vocabulary words from the unit in the correct column. Add any other words that you learned. Circle words you still need to practice.

NOUN	VERB	ADJECTIVE	ADVERB & OTHER

C Reflect on the ideas in the unit as you answer these questions.

1. What did you find most impressive about the Sustainable City in the video?

2. What sustainability initiatives would you like to see in your town or city?

3. What is the most important thing you learned in this unit?

UNIT 7

RETHINKING TOURISM

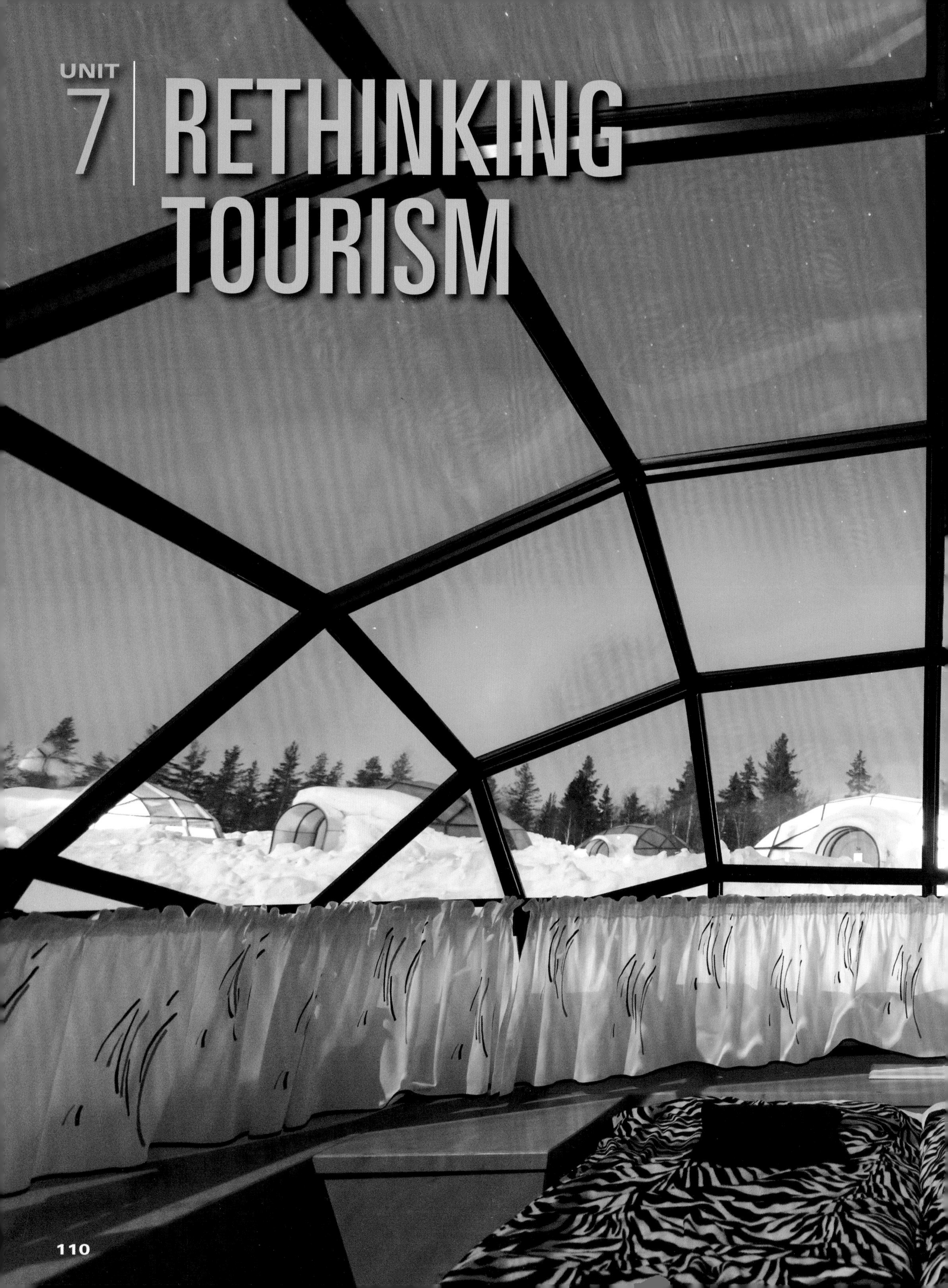

Saariselkä, Finland

CONNECT TO THE TOPIC

1. Where is the woman in the photo? What is she doing?

2. Would you like to have an experience like this?

PREPARE TO WATCH

A VOCABULARY Listen to the words. Read the sentences and write the words that can replace the underlined phrases. Use a dictionary if necessary. ⬛ 7.1

demand (n)	elsewhere (adv)	landlord (n)	occurrence (n)	regulations (n)
dramatic (adj)	isolated (adj)	minimize (v)	promotion (n)	ruin (v)

1. The city leaders have done a lot of <u>market research and advertising</u> to encourage people from other countries to visit. _____

2. The scenery is really <u>striking and exciting</u>, particularly up in the mountains. _____

3. There's an enormous <u>need</u> for new hotels. There aren't enough rooms for everyone who wants to visit. _____

4. In popular tourist areas, a <u>person who rents their house to others</u> can make a lot of money. _____

5. In some places, there are a lot of tourists, but <u>in other places</u>, it's not very developed in terms of tourism. _____

6. There are usually <u>official rules</u> about how to rent out your house online. You can ask your local town government. _____

7. Tourists can easily damage natural places accidentally. We need to <u>reduce to the smallest level</u> the impact tourists have on the wild. _____

8. Bad weather in an area can often <u>spoil or destroy</u> a traveler's vacation. _____

9. It's a very common <u>event</u> to see tourists on the street taking photos of the sites. _____

10. Tourism should be used to create more jobs in areas that are <u>distant and far away from other places</u>. _____

B PERSONLIZE Discuss these questions with a partner.

1. How can you **minimize** errors in your work?
2. What is a **landlord** typically responsible for?
3. **Has** anything ever **ruined** an event, trip, or project for you? What happened?

C Complete the paragraph with the correct form of words from activity A. Then listen and check. 🎧 7.2

The Isle of Skye in the northwest of Scotland has some of the most beautiful and
¹_____ scenery in the UK. It is relatively ²_____ from the rest of the U.K., but the Scottish government has done a lot of ³_____ and there is now huge ⁴_____ to visit the island. Crowds of tourists in the capital, Portree, are a common ⁵_____. Has this saved the tiny island or ⁶_____ it?

REFLECT   Assess the impact of tourism.

You are going to watch a video about tourism on the Isle of Skye. Look at the infographic. What impact, positive and negative, do you think tourism has had on the island? Make a list and share with a partner.

TOURISM ON THE ISLE OF SKYE

The Isle of Skye is an island off the coast of Scotland with a population of 12,000.

Average length of stay
3 nights

Full-time jobs created by tourism 2,850

Total visitor spending
$270,000,000

Positive impact	Negative impact

SPOILING SKYE?

A PHRASES TO KNOW Choose the correct meaning of these phrases from the video.

1. Everyone is **jumping on the bandwagon**.

   a. joining other people in doing something popular

   b. trying to do something better than everybody else

2. No one is **pointing the finger** at you.

   a. talking about you when you are not there

   b. accusing you of doing something bad

3. Local people are **cashing in on** the large number of tourists.

   a. making money from an opportunity

   b. selling things that are not valuable

B MAIN IDEAS Watch the video and check (✓) the ideas that you hear. ▶ 7.1

1. _____ Skye is the most beautiful island in Scotland.

2. _____ Skye has become very popular with tourists in recent years because of social media.

3. _____ Many local people are renting their homes to tourists on Airbnb.

4. _____ The hotels and guest houses are not happy with the situation.

5. _____ Because of renting to tourists, there aren't enough homes for local people.

6. _____ Homeowners make more money renting their homes to tourists than to locals.

7. _____ Local people want fewer tourists to visit the island.

C DETAILS Read the statements. Write T for *True* or F for *False*. The watch the video again. Check your answers and correct the false statements. ▶ 7.1

1. _____ The Isle of Skye is connected to the east coast of Scotland by a bridge.

2. _____ The island became more popular with tourists because of a film festival.

3. _____ There are about 650,000 tourists who visit the island every year.

4. _____ The island has almost 5,000 Airbnb listings.

5. _____ Landlords can charge $100–$300 a night for a house on Airbnb.

6. _____ There are regulations that stop people from renting their houses on Airbnb.

7. _____ David and his wife rent their house to tourists because there is so much demand.

8. _____ There was about an 8 percent increase in tourist rental listings in the area last year.

9. _____ Local people don't want the tourists to stop coming, but they do want a solution to the housing problem.

D Discuss the questions in a small group. Explain your answers.

1. Would you like to visit the Isle of Skye?

2. Should the Isle of Skye introduce regulations to stop homeowners from renting their houses to tourists? If yes, what regulations?

Portree, Isle of Skye, Scotland

PRONUNCIATION   Intonation in short exchanges 🎧7.3

Intonation can add meaning to individual words in short exchanges.
By combining rising and falling intonation, we can indicate a question,
confirmation, enthusiasm, doubt, and other emotions.

A: Happy? ⟋   (questioning)
B: *Definitely.*

A: *Online booking?*
B: Online. ⟍   (confirming)

A: *Good?*
B: Absolutely! ⟍   (enthusiastic yes)

A: *Cheap?*
B: Yes. ⟍⟋   (doubtful)

E APPLY Listen. Check (✓) the meaning you hear for the words in bold. Then
practice the conversations with a partner. 🎧7.4

	Questioning	Confirming	Enthusiastic	Doubtful
1. **A:** Happy? **B: Yes . . .**				
2. **A:** It's great! **B: Great . . .**				
3. **A:** Like it? **B: Wow . . .**				
4. **A:** I really like it. **B:** Really? **A: Really . . .**				
5. **A:** Nice, isn't it? **B: Nice . . .**				
6. **A:** Where did you get it? **B:** Online. **A: Online . . .**				
7. **A:** We're ready. **B: OK . . .**				
8. **A:** Coming? **B: Coming . . .**				

F PRONUNCIATION Work with a partner and create a conversation using short exchanges. Use only a few words on each line with different intonation to show your meaning. Present your conversation to another pair.

A: Need a vacation?

B: _____

A: _____

B: _____

CRITICAL THINKING   Consider an issue from various perspectives

Before deciding if a situation or event has an overall positive or negative impact, it's important to consider the perspectives of the different groups of people who could be impacted. One group may be positively affected while another negatively. To judge the overall impact, it can help to make a list of who will be affected and how.

REFLECT   Consider tourism from various perspectives.

What consequences do high levels of tourism have on different groups of people? Work with a partner and complete the chart. Share your ideas with the class and decide if the overall impact of high levels of tourism is mostly positive or negative.

Impact of high levels of tourism on			
Tourists	Local people who rent their homes	Other local homeowners	Local business owners
crowded sites and attractions			

The Bund,
Shanghai, China

PREPARE TO LISTEN

A VOCABULARY Listen to the words. Then read the definitions and complete the sentences with the words. 🎧 7.5

---

charge (v) to ask for an amount of money for a thing or a service
desire (n) a strong wish for something
dynamic (adj) full of positive energy and ideas
feedback (n) opinions and reactions to a product, service, or experience
host (v) to provide a space for guests and to take care of those guests during their stay
informative (adj) providing knowledge, facts, and details
mainstream (adj) seen as normal and not unusual by most people
nonetheless (adv) despite that; in spite of that
simplify (v) to make less difficult or complicated
specialty (n) a skill that you are very good at or a subject that you know a lot about

---

1. As a tour guide, my job is to show people around and tell them about this town. It has a long and complicated history, but I try to _____ it for the guests on the tour.

2. Most people have some experience with both online shopping and online education. In the past decade, they have become very _____ and not at all unusual.

3. I really learned a lot on the tour. It was very _____.

4. Tourism is good for the economy. For that reason, in many countries there is a strong _____ to attract more tourists.

5. The weather in the area is perfect, there are wonderful sites, and it's not expensive. _____, it's not a popular tourist destination.

6. The tour doesn't cost very much. They only _____ $20 per person.

7. She's a really lively and exciting tour guide. All the guests find her very _____.

8. Over the years, the storyteller has told many different stories, but her _____ is traditional Chinese stories.

9. We are trying to organize a photography exhibition. We've asked the university to _____ it since they have a big hall.

10. Please leave us some _____ about your stay in our hotel. We always like to hear from our guests.

B PERSONALIZE When was the last time you did these things? Tell your partner and give details.

- ▸ left **feedback** online for something that you bought
- ▸ listened to **mainstream** music
- ▸ were **charged** to enter a building
- ▸ listened to an **informative** podcast
- ▸ **hosted** a guest in your house
- ▸ talked to someone who you found very **dynamic**

REFLECT   Reflect on tourism preferences.

You are going to listen to a lecture about new kinds of tourism experiences. Read about three tours. Then discuss these questions in a small group.

1. Which tour would you most like to take, and why?

2. Which tour would work best as an "online experience" that people can enjoy from their computer, tablet, or phone in their own home? Explain.

Swimming in Wadi Shab, Oman | 3 hours
Have you ever had the desire to swim in the desert? On this tour, hosted by our guide Faisal, you hike through the mountains of Oman, then swim to a hidden waterfall. We take care of everything including transportation. So, simplify your trip and book with us!

Montreal Street Art Tour, Canada | 3 hours
Join us on a tour of the streets of Montreal. We will see around 30 works of street art, each between two and nine stories tall. Street art has become more mainstream recently, and your informative tour guide, Beth, will tell you all about it. Check out her five-star feedback!

The Street Food of Bangkok, Thailand | 3 hours
Everybody knows that street food is one of Bangkok's specialties. And on this tour, your dynamic tour guide, Chati, will take you to some of the best street food stalls in the city—on the back of an electric scooter! We don't charge for the tour. You only pay for the food you eat.

LISTEN & SPEAK

ONLINE TOURISM

A PREVIEW What is happening in the photo? Do you think you would enjoy this experience?

Two women host an online tourist experience in the terraced rice fields near Jiache Village, Guizhou Province, China.

B MAIN IDEAS Listen to the lecture. Check (✓) the two main ideas. 🎧 7.6

1. _____ In 2020, many tour companies began to offer online experiences.
2. _____ Most tour companies that tried online tourism in 2020 were successful.
3. _____ Online tourism experiences have been popular for many years.
4. _____ Most tour guides have found it surprisingly easy to offer online tours.
5. _____ The skills needed to be an online tour guide can be learned.
6. _____ Most people find online tours similar to watching videos online.

C DETAILS Choose the correct answers according to the lecture. Then listen again to check your answers. 🎧 7.6

1. Online tourism involves finding out about another part of the world while you are at home, with the help of _____.

   a. videos   b. a local tour guide   c. a guidebook

2. Tour companies moved their experiences online during the pandemic of 2020 because they needed new ways to _____.

   a. make money   b. get feedback   c. go mainstream

3. Tour companies that tested the market with online experiences found that people wanted to _____.

   a. interact with   b. watch videos   c. experience
      other tourists   something new

4. Guides new to online tours have to get used to not _____ guests.

   a. seeing or hearing   b. talking to   c. getting reactions from

5. Often, guides who are new to online tourism find that guests rate the experience as _____ they expect.

   a. worse than   b. the same as   c. better than

6. An online tourism experience is similar to _____.

   a. watching a film   b. attending a concert   c. having a video call

7. In Ricardo's online experience, you learn all about coffee, and you might even see a place in the mountains where coffee is _____.

   a. grown   b. sold   c. packaged

8. If you want to host an online experience, the most important thing is to be _____.

   a. calm   b. detailed   c. dynamic

D DETAILS Check (✓) the correct answers according to the video.

1. In what three ways are online tourism experiences different from watching a video?

   a. _____ The guide has a lot of local knowledge.

   b. _____ The guide makes the experience personal.

   c. _____ The tour experiences are limited in time.

   d. _____ The experiences are live so anything can happen.

   e. _____ Guests can interact with the guide and the other people on the experience.

   f. _____ The experiences are free.

2. What are the three secrets to hosting an online experience?

   a. _____ Try to behave normally in front of the camera.

   b. _____ Talk about a topic that you know a lot about.

   c. _____ Learn how to use the technology.

   d. _____ Make sure the information is detailed.

   e. _____ Make the experience interesting but not too complicated.

   f. _____ Make sure that everyone interacts with each other.

E Would you be good at hosting online experiences? Tell a partner why or why not.

LISTENING SKILL   Listen for rhetorical questions

Rhetorical questions are questions that the speaker does not expect the listener to answer. They can be used for a variety of purposes:

▸ to signal a change in topic

   So, what are the secrets to hosting a successful online experience?

▸ to get the listener thinking or to persuade the listener that an opinion is correct—often in the form of a negative question

   Wouldn't you rather experience something online than not at all?

It's useful to understand when and why the speaker is asking a rhetorical question because it helps you understand what is coming next and how a speaker may be trying to influence your opinion.

F Listen and complete the rhetorical questions. Then choose the purpose of the question. 🎧 7.7

1. _____ the experience?

   a. to signal a change in topic   b. to persuade the listener

2. _____ how to do that?

   a. to signal a change in topic   b. to persuade the listener

Present a plan for an online tourist experience.

You are going to work with other students to create a plan for an online tourist experience. The aim of the experience is to give tourists a "taste" of your country or an area you know well. Use the ideas, vocabulary, and skills from the unit.

G MODEL Listen to a student present plans for an online experience. Complete the chart with the words in the box. Then compare your answers with a partner. 🎧 7.8

apartment   art   dish   gold   imperfection   participant   taste   watch

Title	A ¹_____ of Japan		
Description	a dynamic online experience that introduces guests to the culture, ²_____, and food of Japan		
Location	Shiori's ³_____		
	Host	Plan	Guest activity
Part 1	Shiori	introduce guests to concepts, such as *wabi sabi*—the beauty of ⁴_____	listen and ask questions
Part 2	the speaker	demonstrate *kintsugi*, the art of repairing things with ⁵_____	⁶_____ and chat online
Part 3	Kevin	show how to make *onigiri*, a Japanese ⁷_____	cook along with Kevin
Cost	$5 for each ⁸_____		
Guests will . . .	learn about Japanese culture, try *kintsugi*, and make and taste *onigiri*		

kintsugi bowl

H NOTICE THE GRAMMAR Read the excerpt from the student presentation. Underline three different ways to talk about the future.

We're going to keep the experience affordable, so we'll be charging five dollars for each participant. . . . We hope that it will be an enjoyable experience.

GRAMMAR   Future forms

In English, there are various ways to talk about the future depending on your meaning.

▸ For simple predictions, use *will* / *be going to* + base form of the verb.
  *Our guests **will learn** a little about Japanese culture.*

  *You**'re going to love** the experience.*

▸ For plans and intentions, use *be* + *going to* + base form of the verb.
  *Shiori **is going to talk** about wabi sabi.*

  *We**'re going to host** the experience in her apartment.*

▸ You can use the future continuous (*will be* + verb +*ing* or *be* + *going to be* + verb +*ing*) for plans and intentions as well.
  *We'**ll be charging** five dollars per person.*

  *She**'s going to be taking** the tour tomorrow.*

▸ For a future time clause, use simple present or present continuous—<u>not</u> a future form.
  *<u>While</u> the host <u>is cooking</u>, we **will be watching**.*

  *We**'re going to start** the presentation <u>when</u> everyone <u>arrives</u>.*

▸ For planned events, you can use the present continuous (*be* + verb +*ing*) if it's clear that you are talking about a future time.
  *We **are hosting** our event <u>next Friday</u>.*

  *<u>This afternoon</u> I'**m playing** soccer.*

I   GRAMMAR Choose the correct forms of the verb to complete the sentences. More than one form may be correct.

1. Our online guests _____ all about the Mexican Day of the Dead festival.

   a. are learning   b. are going to learn   c. will be learning

2. While my grandmother _____ guests how to make pasta, they will be making their own pasta at home.

   a. will show   b. is going to show   c. is showing

3. Most likely, we _____ tired by the end of the presentation.

   a. 'll feel   b. 're feeling   c. 'll be feeling

4. Did you know that Vietnam is the second-biggest coffee producer in the world? I _____ more facts just like this during the presentation.

    a. 'm going to give   b. 'll be giving   c. 'm giving

5. It's going to be a great online experience. You _____ a lot.

    a. 'll learn   b. 're going to learn   c. are learning

6. I've ordered a new computer. Hopefully, it will arrive before the first experience _____.

    a. begins   b. is going to begin   c. will begin

7. This time next week, I _____ on the beach. I can't wait for my vacation in the sun!

    a. 'll sit   b. 'm going to be sitting   c. 'll be sitting

8. Before the experience, we _____ guests a list of ingredients that they need.

    a. 're sending   b. 're going to send   c. 'll be sending

9. I _____ class early tomorrow so that I can organize the presentation.

    a. 'm leaving   b. 'm going to leave   c. 'll be leaving

J PERSONALIZE Complete the sentences with your own ideas and discuss with a partner.

1. When I have some free time, _____.

2. If my life goes as planned, five years from now, _____.

3. I won't stop studying English until _____.

SPEAKING SKILL   Give an overview of a presentation

At the start of a presentation, it's useful to give a brief overview of the information you plan to include. This helps your listeners understand what they're going to hear and makes the content of your presentation easier to follow.

First, I'm going to talk about/introduce . . .
Then, I'm planning to show/demonstrate how to . . .
After that, we'll look at/explore . . .
Finally, we'll be taking questions/asking for feedback . . .

K APPLY Listen to the start of another presentation. Match the beginning of each sentence to the ending. 🎧 7.9

1. First, we're going to talk about _____
2. Then, we're planning to discuss _____
3. After that, guests will prepare _____
4. And finally, we will be making _____

a. the pasta at home.
b. a traditional Italian pasta dish.
c. the ingredients and where to buy them.
d. the role of pasta in Italian culture.

L PLAN Work in groups of three. Use the chart to prepare your online experience. Each person in your group should host a different part of the experience. Make sure that guests have a variety of activities to do.

Title			
Description			
Location			
	Host	Plan	Guest activity
Part 1			
Part 2			
Part 3			
Cost			
Guests will learn/see/ experience			

M PRACTICE Practice your presentation in your group. Give each other feedback on how well the presentation is organized. Suggest ways to make it more dynamic.

N UNIT TASK Present your plan for your online experience to another group. Listen to their plan and tell them what you would enjoy about their experience.

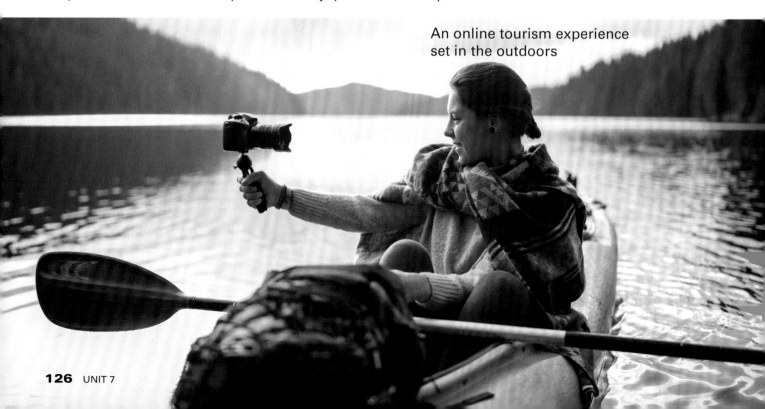

An online tourism experience set in the outdoors

REFLECT

A Check (✓) the Reflect activities you can do and the academic skills you can use.

☐ assess the impact of tourism

☐ consider tourism from various perspectives

☐ reflect on tourism preferences

☐ present a plan for an online tourist experience

☐ listen for rhetorical questions

☐ give an overview of a presentation

☐ future forms

☐ consider an issue from various perspectives

B Write the vocabulary words from the unit in the correct column. Add any other words that you learned. Circle words you still need to practice.

NOUN	VERB	ADJECTIVE	ADVERB & OTHER

C Reflect on the ideas in the unit as you answer these questions.

1. Which place(s) mentioned in this unit would you most like to visit?

_____

_____

2. Overall, do you believe tourism is a good thing or a bad thing?

_____

_____

3. What is the most important thing you learned in this unit?

_____

_____

THE SECRETS OF SUCCESS

Ingvar Moseley prepares for the 110-meter hurdles in Moncton, Canada.

CONNECT TO THE TOPIC

1. Look at the photo. Do you prepare for important events in this way?

2. What are the characteristics of successful teams? What factors can prevent a team from being successful?

PREPARE TO WATCH

A VOCABULARY Listen to the words. Then read the definitions and complete the sentences with the correct form of the words. 🎧 8.1

---

deny (v) to say that something is not true
downside (n) a disadvantage of something
exceptional (adj) very good; much better than usual
extract (v) to remove or take out
force (v) to make someone do something
injury (n) harm or damage to part of the body
intuition (n) a feeling that guides a person about what is right
opponent (n) the person or team that you are playing against
statistics (n) information collected and shown as numbers
tough (adj) difficult or challenging

Imagine you are the coach of a professional sports team. Would you:

1. use data or use your feelings and _____ to decide which players to choose for each game?

2. be demanding and _____ or kind and caring to the players on your team?

3. enjoy the fame of being a top coach or worry about the _____, such as criticism, stress, and pressure?

4. _____ players to train hard every day or allow them to take off one day every week to rest?

5. let players rest if they have a minor _____ after an accident or make them train anyway?

6. encourage the team to respect or to criticize their _____?

7. accept responsibility when the team loses or _____ responsibility and blame the players?

8. look for new players who have incredible talent or players who have a(n) _____ attitude?

9. use feelings or use data and _____ to decide which new players to hire?

10. _____ and analyze information from every game or only from the important games?

B PERSONALIZE Choose five questions from activity A to answer with a partner. Explain your answers.

C Read the job posting and answer the questions.

1. Is this a job that you (or someone you know) would be good at? Explain.
2. If you had to do this job, which sport would you prefer to analyze?

SPORTS DATA SCIENTIST

Data scientist to work for professional sports team. Must have exceptional math skills and be able to analyze data. Love for the tough world of professional sports is an advantage.

Responsibilities include:

- collecting and analyzing data and statistics from games and training
- extracting useful information from data (e.g., when injuries are likely to occur)
- producing reports and recommendations based on data
- analyzing opponents and advising the coach on possible downsides of strategies

APPLY NOW

REFLECT   Consider how data can help a sports team.

You are going to watch a video about the use of data science in professional sports. Work in a small group and list the ways in which data might help a sports team to improve.

—help the coach decide which players to put in the game

Becky Hammon, coach with the San Antonio Spurs, USA

WINNING THROUGH DATA

Fitness skills challenge, Shanghai, China

A MAIN IDEAS Watch the video and take notes in your notebook. ▶ 8.1

B **MAIN IDEAS** Check (✓) the four main ideas that are mentioned in the video. Use your notes.

1. _____ Data has made the National Basketball Association (NBA) more popular.

2. _____ Data is important in the NBA.

3. _____ Data can help prevent injuries.

4. _____ All professional sports teams have data scientists.

5. _____ Data is changing the way sports are played.

6. _____ Data is very expensive to collect and analyze.

7. _____ There are downsides to using data in sports.

C **DETAILS** Watch the video again and choose the correct answers. More than one answer may be possible. ▶ 8.1

1. Every NBA arena has _____.

   a. cameras
   b. data scientists
   c. an American and a Canadian team

2. Data scientists have to _____.

   a. extract useful information
   b. make information understandable
   c. create winning strategies

3. Data scientists study the _____.

   a. team players
   b. team's fans
   c. team's opponents

4. Because of injury, the average professional rugby player _____.

   a. plays two games a season
   b. misses two games a season
   c. misses half a season

5. The New South Wales rugby team used data to decide when to have players rest, resulting in _____ injuries.

   a. fewer
   b. the same number of
   c. more

6. Because of data science, German players in the World Cup in 2014 _____.

   a. were more successful
   b. scored fewer goals
   c. kept the ball for less time

7. Some people say that data science is making the _____.

   a. big name players less popular
   b. coach less important
   c. games more boring

8. Data scientists say that they improve sports for fans by showing them _____.

   a. which strategies work
   b. how to better understand games
   c. how to make games faster

D PHRASES TO KNOW Work with a partner. Discuss the meaning of these phrases from the video. Then say if you agree with each statement and why.

1. I am the kind of person who **takes the lead** in challenging situations.

2. If it's offered helpfully, we should **take** criticism **to heart**.

3. There are many benefits to competing in sports. **Take, for example**, statistics that show students in athletics often have better grades.

GRAMMAR   Gerunds/infinitives as subjects; preposition + gerund

Gerunds (verb + -*ing*) and gerund phrases can be the subject of a sentence. Gerund subjects are always singular.

> **Making data understandable** _is_ part of the data scientist's job.

> **Motivating players** _is_ something only the coach can do.

Gerunds and gerund phrases also follow prepositions, such as *before*, *in*, *on*, and *to* (not to be confused with the infinitive *to*).

> Data has become essential _in_ **training individual players**.

> _Before_ **introducing the new strategy**, they analyzed a lot of data.

> I'm looking forward _to_ **competing**.

Infinitives (*to* + verb) and infinitive phrases follow *It* + *be* + adjectives.

> _It's easy_ **to see why fans don't like it**.

> _It's important for any team_ **to know how to improve**.

An infinitive can also be a subject, but it is not common. We prefer to use *It* + adjective + infinitive.

> NOT COMMON: **To know how to improve** is important for any team.

E GRAMMAR Complete the sentences with the gerund or infinitive form of the verb in parentheses.

1. I'm worried about _____ against her. She's so good! (play)

2. It's important _____ whichever sport you play. (enjoy)

3. _____ a soccer club as a child changed my life. (join)

4. _____ a pro involves practicing hard every day. (be)

5. It's impossible for me _____ who is going to win the World Series. (guess)

6. Passion and _____ to win are common characteristics of professional athletes. (want)

7. It's not very smart _____ when you are injured. (exercise)

8. How did you get so good at _____ the ball? (throw)

F GRAMMAR Complete the sentences with a gerund or infinitive phrase. Then compare your sentences with a partner.

Biting my nails is a really annoying habit of mine. I'd like to stop doing it.

1. _____ is a really annoying habit of mine. I'd like to stop doing it.

2. _____ is one of my passions, and I'm very good at it.

3. It's not easy _____. In fact, it's much harder than learning English.

4. _____ would be my dream come true. I've always wanted to do it.

5. I'm looking forward to _____ next weekend.

6. When I lie awake at night, I often think about _____.

7. If you want to speak English well, it's important _____.

8. It's unusual for me _____.

9. I'm afraid of _____.

10. _____ is one of my favorite things to do.

CRITICAL THINKING   Relate concepts to your experience

Some concepts can seem abstract until we relate them to our personal lives. Seeing the personal connection helps to make the concept understandable, memorable, and relevant. When you learn about a new idea or concept, take some time to think about how it might apply to your life. List the ways in which it relates to you or has an impact on you.

REFLECT   Discuss how data can improve your life.

1. Check (✓) the kinds of data that you currently track or follow. Put an X for the data you would like to track that you don't currently. Add more kinds of data, if possible.

   _____ distance walked per day   _____ money earned   _____ blood pressure

   _____ screen time   _____ calories burned   _____ stress levels

   _____ calories consumed   _____ cups of coffee per day _____ _____

   _____ hours of sleep   _____ minutes of exercise   _____ _____

   _____ hours spent working   _____ money spent   _____ _____

2. Compare with a partner and discuss the questions.

   a. How do you track this data?

   b. How does it help you?

   c. How would tracking other data improve your life?

PREPARE TO LISTEN

A **VOCABULARY** Listen to the words. Read the sentences and write the words that can replace the underlined phrases. Use a dictionary if necessary. 🎧 8.2

anxiety (n)	consequently (adv)	coordinate (v)	overwhelming (adj)	pressure (n)
bonus (n)	consistent (adj)	doubt (v)	paralyzed (adj)	state (n)

1. I try to be <u>sure to always do the same thing</u> in my weekly fitness routine. I do one run, one swim, and one yoga session every week. _____

2. Once my friend climbed up to the highest diving board at our local swimming pool. When he got to the top, he was so scared that he was <u>unable to move</u>. _____

3. When I speak English with someone outside of class, I find it stressful. I start to <u>feel uncertain about</u> my skills, and this doesn't help me to speak fluently. _____

4. I got an F for a college paper I wrote recently. I didn't expect that, so I was upset and in a bad <u>condition</u> after I got the paper back. _____

5. Professional soccer players often get a <u>reward of extra money</u> if they win a competition. _____

6. When I was young, I had a part in our school play. When I saw all the people in the audience, I found it <u>stressful and I was unable to think clearly,</u> and I started to cry! _____

7. I tried playing basketball when I was younger, but I couldn't <u>make</u> my arms and legs <u>work together</u>. I couldn't run while bouncing the ball. I was hopeless! _____

8. My dad was a champion ice skater, and he really wanted me to be good at ice skating. That created a lot of <u>uncertainty and nervousness</u> about skating for me. _____

9. Playing games makes me competitive. <u>As a result</u>, I get angry if I lose. _____

10. My father is a professor, and my mother is a lawyer. For this reason, there was <u>a strong expectation and demand</u> for me to do well in school. _____

B **PERSONALIZE** Check (✓) the experiences that you have had recently. Tell your partner about the experiences.

_____ found a project or task **overwhelming**

_____ felt in a **state** of shock

_____ felt **pressure** from your peers

_____ felt **anxiety**

_____ felt **paralyzed** by **doubt**

C How do you feel when you are under pressure? Look at the infographic. Work with a partner and add one or two more symptoms to each category.

Under Pressure?

PHYSICAL SYMPTOMS

- Increased heart rate
- _____
- _____

EMOTIONAL SYMPTOMS

- Feeling overwhelmed
- _____
- _____

BEHAVIORAL SYMPTOMS

- Biting nails
- _____
- _____

COGNITIVE SYMPTOMS

- Inability to focus
- _____
- _____

REFLECT Examine how you respond to pressure.

Before you listen to a lecture about athletes who perform poorly during high pressure situations, complete the tasks.

1. Read the situations below and rank them in order for you.
   1 = causes the most anxiety, 6 = causes the least anxiety

   _____ public speaking   _____ an important exam

   _____ performing in a talent show   _____ a job interview

   _____ an argument with a neighbor   _____ an important team game

2. Explain your answers to a partner. What symptoms would you experience?

3. What techniques do you use or know about to cope with high pressure situations?

NO TIME TO CHOKE

A MAIN IDEAS Listen and take notes. Choose the correct answers. 🎧 8.3

1. Choking is when a professional athlete _____ in a high pressure situation.

   a. performs much worse than normal

   b. tries too hard

   c. finds that they can't move at all

2. The thing that causes a top athlete to choke is _____.

   a. sweating and a high heart rate

   b. a failure to manage anxiety

   c. not using their brain

3. In order to prevent choking, there is/are _____ a professional athlete can do.

   a. nothing

   b. one simple thing

   c. several things

Canadian Valérie Maltais falls at the 2018 Olympics in PyeongChang, South Korea.

B DETAILS Listen again and choose the correct answers. 🎧 8.3

1. Allan Donald lost the game for South Africa because he was unable to _____.

   a. hit the ball far enough   b. run when he needed to   c. turn around

2. In normal life, if you are choking, _____.

   a. something is blocking   b. you are thinking about   c. you are not performing well
      your breathing   breathing too much

3. An example of choking is when, at an important moment, a golfer _____.

   a. misses a difficult shot   b. misses an easy shot   c. never misses a shot

4. In soccer tournaments, well-known players are more likely to choke because they _____.

   a. want to win too much   b. fear the other team   c. are worried about losing respect

5. You start to sweat, your heart rate goes up, and you start to doubt yourself when you _____.

   a. feel anxiety   b. do things you find easy   c. can't coordinate your feet

6. Anxiety causes athletes to _____.

   a. stop thinking   b. think naturally   c. think too much

7. In the world of business, a bigger bonus may cause an employee to _____.

   a. underperform   b. overperform   c. perform as normal

8. In the state of flow, we _____.

   a. feel confident and   b. overthink everything   c. always achieve our goal
      can concentrate   we try to do

9. In order to find a state of flow, you need a consistent routine, the ability to perform under pressure, and the ability to _____.

   a. push the next thing out   b. think deeply about why   c. recover when things
      of your mind   something went wrong   go wrong

C PHRASES TO KNOW With a partner, discuss the meaning of these words from the lecture. Then complete the sentences with the correct form of the words.

overestimate	overthink	underperform

1. The team missed the basket every time they took a shot. They usually play much better, but they really _____ in that game.

2. I spent hours trying to imagine what my opponent would do and how I would respond. I was exhausted. That's when I realized that I was _____ the problem.

3. He had expected to lose, but in fact he won easily. Maybe he _____ his opponent.

D Work with a partner and think of examples of how to apply the techniques to avoid being overwhelmed by anxiety from the lecture to an oral exam in English.

TIP 1: Follow a consistent routine.

Example: _____

_____

TIP 2: Get used to performing under pressure.

Example: _____

_____

TIP 3: Recover when something goes wrong.

Example: _____

_____

LISTENING SKILL   Identify essential information

In exams, you often have to listen to a short lecture and then summarize it. In order to do this, you need to **identify the essential information** to include in your summary. Listen for the following:

1. Signal phrases

   It's important to note that . . .

   The important thing here is . . .

2. Rhetorical questions

   So, what causes athletes to choke and what can the rest of us learn from it?

3. Pace, stress, and intonation that highlight essential information. For example, the speaker may slow down or use exaggerated stress and intonation.

   *The **first** thing you need is a con**sis**tent rou**tine**.*

E **APPLY** Listen to excerpts from a lecture. Check (✓) the technique that the speaker uses to show that the information is essential. 🎧 8.4

	Signal phrase	Rhetorical question	Pace, stress, intonation
1. One-third of students have trouble dealing with anxiety.			
2. People don't respond in the same way to pressure.			
3. One type of stress is called chronic anxiety.			

Supporters cheer on Ecuadorean cyclist Richard Carapaz in Tulcán, Ecuador.

UNIT TASK Summarize a presentation on athletic performance.

You are going to summarize a presentation on how athletes perform well under pressure. Use the ideas, vocabulary, and skills from the unit.

F MODEL Listen to a short lecture about a technique to improve performance in sports. Complete the notes as you listen. 🎧 8.5

Topic	Visualization
Description	1_____ that they are performing an action 2_____ about doing it in the mind first
Other key information	▶ athlete needs to be alone and in 3_____ space ▶ needs to be done many times
First example	pro golfer visualizing hitting ball
Important detail(s)	▶ will visualize all the 4_____ ▶ helps perform the action in real life
Second example	pro ice skater visualizing a jump
Important detail(s)	▶ helps build 5_____

G MODEL Now listen to a student summarizing the lecture. Check your answers in activity F. 🎧 8.6

Qhouirunnisa' Endang Wahyudi performs a football trick in Shah Alam, Selangor, Malaysia.

SPEAKING SKILL   Summarize a lecture

Follow these steps when you summarize a lecture or presentation.

State the topic	*The topic of the presentation is . . .*
Define the topic	*It refers to . . .*
	It involves . . .
Give key information	*It is important to note that . . .*
	The speaker emphasizes that . . .
Give examples	*The first/second example that the speaker gives is . . .*
	Here, . . . / In this example, . . .

H APPLY Listen again to the student summarizing the lecture. Complete the summary with the words that she uses. 🎧 8.6

The topic of the presentation is visualization. Visualization

¹_____ a technique that can help athletes improve their

performance. It ²_____ imagining that they are performing an

action in their minds. They think about doing the action.

³_____ that athletes need to be alone and in a quiet space when they visualize. And ⁴_____ that they need to visualize the action many times.

The first example that the speaker gives is a golfer who imagines hitting a golf ball. ⁵_____, the golfer visualizes all the steps. This helps them feel how the action happens and so helps them perform it in real life.

The second example is an ice skater who imagines doing a difficult jump. ⁶_____, visualization helps the skater build confidence.

PRONUNCIATION Thought groups and intonation 🎧 8.7

Thought groups are groups of words that belong together and express an idea or thought. Each thought group usually has a focus word—which is given more stress—and a slight pause at the end. The intonation is usually higher on the focus word and then falls until the end of the thought group.

You can choose which word to focus on depending on what information you want to emphasize.

Athletes need to be / in a quiet **space** / when they **visualize**.

Athletes **need** to be / in a **quiet** space / when they **visualize**.

I PRONUNCIATION Listen and underline the focus word in each thought group. Then listen again and repeat the sentences. 🎧 8.8

1. Another good way / to deal with pressure / is to talk to yourself / in your head.

2. Regular exercise / can help normal people / deal with anxiety / in their everyday lives.

3. Too much caffeine / causes higher levels of stress, / and it's often better / to drink less.

4. Analyzing yourself / and recognizing the thoughts / that cause you anxiety / can help a lot.

J PRONUNCIATION Practice saying this excerpt from a lecture with a partner. Think about where there are logical thought groups and focus words. Then listen and compare. 🎧 8.9

The third thing you need is the ability to recover when something goes wrong—and it's inevitable that things will go wrong. When they do, you quickly analyze what happened and why, then you push it out of your mind and focus on the next thing.

K PLAN Listen to another lecture and take notes in the chart. 🎧 8.10

Topic	The clutch state
Description	
Other key information	
First example	
Important details	
Second example	
Important details	

L PRACTICE Practice summarizing the lecture in your head. Think about the phrases and pronunciation that you will use to emphasize essential information.

M UNIT TASK Work with a partner and take turns summarizing the lecture. Use your notes to help you. As you listen to your partner, check (✓) what you hear in the summary. Give your partner advice on how to improve the summary.

_____ A clear definition of the topic   _____ Key vocabulary from the unit

_____ Key information about the topic   _____ Phrases from the Speaking Skill box

_____ Summaries of both examples   _____ Use of thought groups and focus words

Dutch cyclist Mathieu van der Poel celebrates a win in Ostend, Belgium.

REFLECT

A Check (✓) the Reflect activities you can do and the academic skills you can use.

- ☐ consider how data can help a sports team
- ☐ discuss how data can improve your life
- ☐ examine how you respond to pressure
- ☐ summarize a presentation on athletic performance

- ☐ identify essential information
- ☐ summarize a lecture
- ☐ gerunds/infinitives as subjects; preposition + gerund
- ☐ relate concepts to your experience

B Write the vocabulary words from the unit in the correct column. Add any other words that you learned. Circle words you still need to practice.

NOUN	VERB	ADJECTIVE	ADVERB & OTHER

C Reflect on the ideas in the unit as you answer these questions.

1. What is the most important thing you learned in this unit?

_____

_____

2. What did you learn about the secrets of success?

_____

_____

3. What techniques to achieve success will you use in the future?

_____

_____

Prefix *over-*

A prefix comes at the beginning of some words. You can add the prefix **over-** to some adjectives, verbs, and nouns to mean "too much" or "more than normal."

*The school has been **over**crowded for years.* = too crowded
*We **over**cooked dinner.* = to cook too much
***Over**work can cause stress and lead to health problems.* = too much work

A Complete each sentence with the correct form of a word from the box and *over-*. One word is extra.

confident (adj)	eat (v)	flow (v)	pay (v)	spend (v)
due (adj)	estimate (v)	load (v)	reaction (n)	time (n)

1. There was so much rain that the river _____ its banks and flooded the town.

2. During your first year in college, it's not a good idea to _____ your schedule. Don't take too many classes.

3. I apologize for getting so angry. It was an _____ to a rather small problem.

4. Your assignment is _____. You should have turned it in last week.

5. Some companies _____ their top executives, while the other employees make an average salary.

6. I usually work 40 hours each week. However, this month I'm working _____ because we're so busy.

7. People tend to _____ on holidays because there is so much good food available.

8. James was _____ about the test material and unfortunately didn't study enough.

9. We _____ the time it would take to finish the project. We completed it in half that time.

B Answer the questions.

1. Have you ever **overreacted** to a situation? Why?

2. Is being **overconfident** ever a problem?

3. Do you ever **overspend**? What do you **overspend** on?

4. Is it common to work **overtime** in your country?

Word roots *struct* and *man*

Many words in English are formed from Latin and Greek word roots. Knowing the meaning of these word roots can help you understand the meaning of unfamiliar vocabulary.

The word root **man** comes from Latin and means "hand."
The word root **struct** comes from Latin and means "build."

A Read the sentences and answer the questions about the words in bold.

1. Homes and buildings around the world are **constructed** out of different materials. What materials are used to **construct** homes in your area?

   _____

2. The **structure** of a skyscraper relies on metal and glass. What creates the **structure** of an organization?

   _____

3. Parents, teachers, and those in charge often **instruct** others. How is **instructing** similar to building?

   _____

4. Natural disasters like hurricanes, earthquakes, and fires can be very **destructive.** In what ways are they **destructive**?

   _____

5. In early 2021, a container ship caused an **obstruction** to the Suez Canal and no other ships could get through. What does an **obstruction** do?

   _____

6. Sometimes people get **manicures** for a special occasion, when they want to look good. What is a **manicure**?

   _____

7. People who do **manual** work get more injuries than those in office jobs. What are some examples of **manual** work?

   _____

8. Video games often require players to **manipulate** buttons or levers on devices. What does it mean to **manipulate** something?

   _____

9. Writers need to turn in a **manuscript** to an editor. Nowadays they are written on a computer, but how were **manuscripts** written a hundred years ago?

   _____

Using a dictionary Synonyms

Many words have synonyms, or words that are similar in meaning. In a dictionary, a synonym may be set in a box labeled *Thesaurus* or marked with *SYN.* You can also look for synonyms in a thesaurus, which usually has a longer list of synonyms or near-synonyms.

deadly (adj.) **1** so dangerous as to cause death: *deadly weapons, deadly poison*
2 *fig.* destructive, terrible

THESAURUS

deadly 1 lethal, fatal, poisonous **2** mean, awful

A Use a dictionary. For each word, find a synonym that is also a word from the unit.

1. bacteria (n) _____

2. standard (n) _____

3. stage (n) _____

4. sanitation (n) _____

5. perspire (v) _____

6. heal (v) _____

7. direct (adj) _____

8. fatal (adj) _____

B Answer the questions using a synonym for the word in bold.

1. What is an example of a **deadly** disease?

   _____

2. Is it always good to be **straightforward** with people? Explain.

   _____

3. Why are the teenaged years a stressful **phase** for many people?

   _____

4. How can we prevent **germs** from spreading?

   _____

Word roots *funct* and *spir*

Many words in English are formed from Latin and Greek word roots. Knowing the meaning of these word roots can help you understand the meaning of unfamiliar vocabulary.

The word root **funct** comes from Latin and means "perform" or "purpose."
The word root **spir** comes from Latin and means "breathe" or "to have a desire for."

Sometimes a word will not have the exact meaning of the word root, but there will be a figurative or symbolic connection.

A Match the words in bold to their definitions.

a. (n) a failure to work properly
b. (v) to seek to accomplish
c. (adj) having many uses or purposes
d. (adj) no longer existing
e. (v) to act together in secret, usually to do something illegal
f. (adj) not having a use or purpose
g. (n) the action of sweating
h. (n) breathing
i. (n) the inner quality or nature of someone

_____ 1. **Perspiration** helps cool the body. The water lowers the skin's temperature

_____ 2. The fireplace is **nonfunctional**. It's not connected to a chimney, so don't try to light a fire!

_____ 3. Severe allergies can sometimes affect **respiration** and must be treated immediately.

_____ 4. Jeong **aspires** to run a company one day, so she's taking business classes.

_____ 5. The large room at the end of the hall is **multifunctional**. We can hold meetings there, but employees can also use it as an individual workspace.

_____ 6. I worked for 20 years at a company that is now **defunct**. It went out of business two years ago.

_____ 7. Several well-known politicians were arrested. They **conspired** to steal public money.

_____ 8. There was a **malfunction** with the voting machines, so the votes had to be counted by hand.

_____ 9. People are attracted to Halima because she has such a joyful **spirit.**

Suffix *-ous*

You can add the suffix **-ous** to some nouns to make adjectives. This suffix means "full of," "like," or "having the quality of."

*I've always thought my brother was very humor**ous**.*

If the noun ends in *-y,* change the *y* to and *i* and then add *-ous.* If the word ends in an *-e,* the *e* sometimes is dropped, and sometimes is changed. There are exceptions to these rules. If you are not sure, check the spelling in a dictionary.

*humor + **ous** = humor**ous***
*env~~y~~ + **ous** = env**ious***
*ridicul~~e~~ + **ous** = ridicul**ous***

A Complete each conversation with the correct adjective form. Use a noun from the box and *-ous.* Two words are extra. Check your spelling in a dictionary.

adventure	anxiety	courage	disaster	industry	outrage
ambition	caution	courtesy	fury	luxury	space

1. A: Emma has a(n) _____ plan to start her own company. She has big dreams.

    B: I hope she is _____ then. Starting a company is very hard work.

2. A: I thought Henry's behavior was really _____! He was very rude to you.

    B: I know. I was _____ at first, but I'm feeling less angry now.

3. A: Are you _____ about your job interview?

    B: Yes, I am. The last interview was _____. I can't believe it was such a failure.
    I'm worried it might happen again.

4. A: I really admire Miguel. I think he's _____. I'm not as brave as he is.

    B: I know what you mean. I am much more _____. I try to avoid risks.

5. A: You moved to a bigger apartment, didn't you? Is it much more _____?

    B: Yes, it's huge! And everything is much nicer. It's really _____.

B Answer the questions.

1. How important is it to be **courteous** to others? Explain.

    _____

2. What might an **adventurous** person do on a trip or vacation?

    _____

3. Which of the qualities from activity A do you most want to have? Why?

    _____

Using a dictionary Word families

A dictionary will often identify words in the same family. It will show the base word and a list of words with various suffixes added that change the part of speech.

sustainable (adj) involving the use of methods that don't harm the environment
- sustainability (n)
- sustainably (adv)

Dictionaries also allow you to look at nearby words, which may belong to the same family.

ideal (adj) perfect, the best something can be
idealist (n) one who has high ideals
idealistic (adj) wishing for perfection

A Use a dictionary to find other words in these word families. There may be more than one related word for some parts of speech.

Noun	Verb	Adjective	Adverb
	argue		
authority			
		economic	
maintenance			
	propose		
		sensible	
	signify		

B Complete the sentences with words in the word families from activity A.

1. The mayor or city council has to _____ new construction in the downtown area. Builders need that permission first.

2. Unfortunately, the building has been poorly _____ and now requires many repairs.

3. One way to _____ is to reduce energy costs. Even turning off lights can help.

4. In our _____, we suggest ways to improve sustainability.

5. Her _____ was not very convincing. She should support her opinion with more facts.

6. After construction began, the design changed _____ from the original one.

Compound words

Compound words are formed when two or more words are joined together to make a new word. You can often use the meaning of the individual words to determine the meaning of the compound. Compound words can be single words, hyphenated words, or two words. Check the spelling in a dictionary.

elsewhere
one word

self-confidence
hyphenated word

ice cream
two words

A Think about the meanings of the individual words in these compounds. Then write each compound word next to its definition.

Common compounds

self-conscious, self-centered, self-service   workplace, hardworking, paperwork
lifetime, lifestyle, wildlife   landmark, mainland, woodland

1. _____ (n) the period of time that someone is alive

2. _____ (n) an area covered with trees

3. _____ (adj) concerned only with one's own interests

4. _____ (n) routine record-keeping, often less important than other tasks

5. _____ (n) a particular way of life

6. _____ (n) a place of employment

7. _____ (adj) productive, regularly engaged in serious work

8. _____ (n) serving oneself, for example, food at a restaurant

9. _____ (n) animals living in their natural setting

10. _____ (n) land on a continent, not including islands

11. _____ (n) an object on land that is easily seen or recognized

12. _____ (adj) worried about what others think of you

B Complete the sentences with the correct form of the words from activity A.

1. The Orkney Islands are off the coast of Scotland. Visitors can take a boat from the _____ of Scotland to Orkney to see whales, birds and other _____.

2. It would take a _____ to see all of China, but, even on a brief visit, you can visit many of the most famous _____.

3. I think I'm a _____ employee, but there's simply too much _____. I'd prefer a _____ with more fun and challenge.

Prefixes *co-/con-* and *ex-*

You can add prefixes to some words or word roots to change their meaning.
Co- and **con-** usually mean "with" or "together."

> *coordinate* = to make something work together
> *consistent* = done in the same way over time, in agreement with

Ex- often means "from" or "out."

> *exception(al)* = out of the ordinary, unusual
> *extract* = to remove or take out

When you see a new word beginning with these prefixes, you have a clue to help you understand the meaning.

A Choose the correct answers.

1. To *inhabit* means to live in a place. Who or what might *cohabit*?

    a. fish and birds   b. colleagues   c. a married couple

2. To *import* means to bring something in. What does *export* probably mean?

    a. to send something out   b. to carry something   c. to hold something up
                                   across

3. Your birthday party is next week. You probably want to *include* your family members. Who do you want to *exclude?*

    a. friends   b. strangers   c. classmates

4. I need a new passport. What probably happened to the old one?

    a. It inspired.   b. It conspired.   c. It expired.

5. If someone *exclaims* in surprise, what do they do?

    a. cry out   b. move away   c. take a breath

6. The two scientists are *co-authors* of the report. What did they do?

    a. argued in the report   b. sent out the report   c. wrote the report together

7. Parents need to give their *consent* for their children to go on a school trip. What does *consent* probably mean?

    a. agreement, permission   b. refusal   c. money

8. When you move to a new culture, it's a good idea to *conform* to the customs. What does *conform* probably mean?

    a. accept fully   b. act in agreement   c. learn

VOCABULARY INDEX

Unit 1	Page	CEFR	Unit 3	Page	CEFR
climax	4	OFF	advertisers	46	OFF
conflict*	4	B2	attain*	40	C1
crisis	4	B2	belief	46	B2
crush	10	C2	claim	46	B2
dilemma*	4	B2	concept*	46	B2
entire	10	B2	cure*	40	B2
exhaustion	10	B2	deadly	46	B2
flaw	4	C1	design*	46	B1
incident*	4	B2	germs	46	C1
lean	10	B2	historically*	40	C1
moral	4	B2	hygiene	40	C1
obstacle	4	C1	infection	46	B2
overcome	4	B2	medical*	40	B2
platform	10	B2	norm*	40	C1
roar	10	C2	phase*	46	B2
sniff*	10	C2	rub*	40	B2
stab	10	B2	spread	46	B2
status*	4	C1	straightforward*	40	B2
trip over	10	B2	sweat	40	B2
weapon	10	B2	treat	40	B2

Unit 2	Page	CEFR	Unit 4	Page	CEFR
accelerate*	22	C1	bond*	58	B2
approach*	28	B2	complex*	64	B2
brand	22	B2	constantly*	58	B2
chemicals*	22	B2	diverse*	64	B2
clothing	22	B2	drought	58	C2
cost	22	B2	fire	64	B2
destruction	22	B2	function*	58	B2
discard	28	OFF	hire	64	B2
edible	28	C1	humility	64	C2
emissions*	22	C1	impact*	58	B2
fabric*	22	C1	initiate*	58	C2
gallon	22	OFF	inspiration	64	B2
generate*	28	B2	numerous	64	C1
manufacture	22	B2	observe	58	B2
peer	28	C1	predator*	58	C1
profitable	28	B2	reorganize	64	C1
simply	28	B2	role*	58	B2
tackle	28	B2	satisfaction	64	B2
toxic*	28	B2	target*	64	B2
turnover	28	C1	threat	58	B2

*Academic words

VOCABULARY INDEX

NOTE-TAKING SKILLS

Taking clear notes will improve your understanding and retention of the ideas you hear. Because you need to interpret your own notes, it's important to develop a system that works for you. However, there are some common strategies to improve your note taking.

BEFORE YOU LISTEN

▸ Focus: Try to clear your mind before the speaker begins so you can pay attention. If possible, review previous notes or think about what you already know about the topic.

▸ Predict: If you know the topic of the talk, think about what you might hear.

WHILE YOU LISTEN

▸ Take notes by hand: Research suggests that taking notes by hand rather than on a computer is more effective. Taking notes by hand requires you to summarize, rephrase, and synthesize information. This helps you encode the information (put it into a form that you can understand and remember).

▸ Listen for organizational clues: Speakers often use organizational clues (e.g., *We'll start by . . ., then . . ., and finally . . .*) to organize their ideas and show relationships between them. Listening for organizational clues can help you decide what information to write in your notes. For example, if you hear "There are three important factors to consider," you can write 1–3 so that you are ready to take note of the three factors.

▸ Condense (shorten) information:

  • As you listen, focus on the most important ideas. The speaker will usually repeat, define, explain, and/or give examples of these ideas. Take notes on these ideas.

  • Don't write full sentences. Write only key words (nouns, verbs, adjectives, and adverbs), phrases, or short sentences.

  • Leave out information that is obvious.

  • Write numbers and statistics using numerals (e.g., *9 bil; 35%*).

  • Use abbreviations (e.g., *ft., min., yr.*) and symbols (=, ≠, >, <, %, →).

  • Use indenting to show different levels of importance. Write main ideas on the left side of the paper. Indent details.

  • Write details under key terms to help you remember them.

  • Write the definitions of important new words.

AFTER YOU LISTEN

▸ Review your notes soon after the lecture or presentation. Add any details you missed.

▸ Clarify anything you don't understand in your notes with a classmate or teacher.

▸ Add or highlight main ideas. Cross out details that aren't important or necessary.

▸ Rewrite anything that is hard to read or understand. Rewrite your notes in an outline or other graphic organizer to organize the information more clearly.

▸ Use arrows, boxes, diagrams, or other visual cues to show relationships between ideas.

ORGANIZING INFORMATION

You can use a graphic organizer to take notes while you are listening, or to organize your notes after you listen. Here are some examples of graphic organizers.

FLOWCHARTS are used to show processes, or cause/effect relationships.

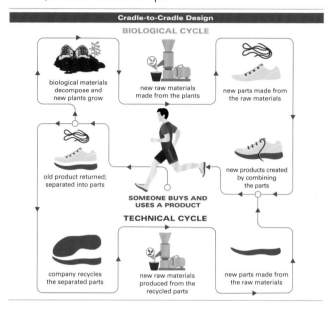

OUTLINES show the relationship between main ideas and details. You can make an outline as you listen or go back and rewrite your notes as an outline later.

First main point: _____

    Supporting info: _____

Second main point: _____

    Supporting info: _____

Third main point: _____

    Supporting info: _____

Conclusion: _____

MIND MAPS show the connection between concepts. The main idea is usually in the center with supporting ideas and details around it.

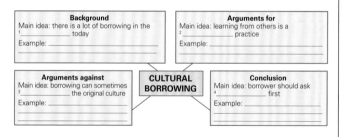

VENN DIAGRAMS compare and contrast two or more topics. The overlapping areas show similarities.

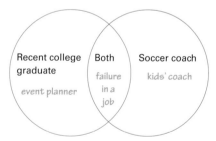

TIMELINES show a sequence of events.

T-CHARTS compare two topics.

Clarifying/checking your understanding

So are you saying that. . .?
So what you mean is. . .?
What do you mean?
How so?
I'm not sure I understand/follow.
Do you mean. . .?
I'm not sure what you mean.

Asking for clarification/confirming understanding

I'm not sure I understand the question.
I'm not sure I understand what you mean.
Sorry, I'm not following you.
Are you saying that. . .?
If I understand correctly, you're saying that. . .

Checking others' understanding

Does that make sense?
Do you understand?
Do you see what I mean?
Is that clear?
Are you following/with me?
Do you have any questions?

Asking for opinions

What do you think?
Do you have anything to add?
What are your thoughts?
How do you feel?
What's your opinion?

Taking turns

Can/May I say something?
Could I add something?
Can I just say. . .?
May I continue?
Can I finish what I was saying?
Did you finish your thought?
Let me finish.

Interrupting politely

Excuse me.
Pardon me.
Forgive me for interrupting. . .
I hate to interrupt, but. . .
Can I stop you for a second?

Asking for repetition

Could you say that again?
I'm sorry?
I didn't catch what you said.
I'm sorry. I missed that. What did you say?
Could you repeat that, please?

Showing interest

I see. Good for you.
Really? Seriously?
Um-hmm. No kidding!
Wow. And? (Then what?)
That's funny/amazing/incredible/awful!

Giving reasons or causes

Because/Since + (clause)
Because of/Due to + (noun phrase)
The reason is (that) + (clause)
One reason is (that) + (clause)
The main reason is (that) + (clause)

Giving results or effects

. . ., so + (clause)
Therefore,/As a result,/Consequently, + (sentence)
. . . causes/leads to + (noun phrase)
. . . had an impact/effect on + (noun phrase)
If + (clause), then + (clause),

Identifying a side track

On a different subject, . . .
As an aside, . . .
That reminds me, . . .
This is off-topic, but . . .

Returning to a previous topic

Getting back to our previous discussion, . . .
To return to our earlier topic, . . .
So, to return to what we were saying, . . .
OK, getting back on topic, . . .

INDEX OF EXAM SKILLS & TASKS

Reflect is designed to provide practice for standardized exams, such as IELTS and TOEFL. This book has many activities that focus on and practice skills and question types that are needed for test success.

LISTENING • Key Skills	IELTS	TOEFL	Page(s)
Listen for gist or main ideas	x	x	7, 8, 9, 13, 14, 25, 31, 42, 49, 61, 67, 79, 84, 96, 103, 114, 121, 132, 133, 138
Listen for key details or examples	x	x	7, 14, 26, 31, 42, 49, 62, 68, 69, 85, 97, 103, 115, 121, 122, 133, 139
Take notes	x	x	18, 25, 26, 36, 51, 54, 67, 87, 90, 99, 108, 132, 138, 141, 144
Predict what you might hear	x	x	13, 42, 61, 66, 102
Preview a topic	x	x	6, 48, 120
Infer meaning	x	x	61
Listen for numbers and figures	x	x	26
Recognize connectors	x	x	86
Match information to a speaker	x	x	25
Listen for sources of information	x	x	44
Listen for rhetorical questions	x	x	122
Identify essential information	x	x	140

LISTENING • Common Question Types	IELTS	TOEFL	Page(s)
Complete a table, chart, notes, or diagram	x		7, 9, 14, 15, 25, 26, 45, 51, 99, 105, 123, 141, 144
Complete sentences, a paragraph, or a summary	x		8, 14, 31, 33, 67, 79, 80, 97, 98, 142
Multiple choice	x	x	7, 14, 42, 44, 49, 96, 121, 138, 139
Multiple response	x	x	49, 67, 68, 69, 114, 121, 122, 133
Match information to a category or person	x	x	31, 61, 79, 84, 116, 140
Short answer	x		85
Put information that you hear in order		x	86
Match beginnings and endings of sentences	x		125

SPEAKING • Key Skills	IELTS	TOEFL	Page(s)
Use appropriate intonation and stress	x	x	35, 50, 71, 89, 116, 117, 143
Discuss problems and solutions	x	x	69, 72, 76, 77, 99, 101, 108
Discuss pros and cons	x	x	23, 95, 113, 117
Make predictions	x	x	27, 31, 42, 66
Summarize a lecture		x	142, 144
Speak in thought groups	x	x	17, 143
Describe trends	x		71, 72
Express personal opinions	x	x	47, 68
Compare two things or ideas	x	x	51, 54
Discuss contrasting information	x	x	88
Brainstorm ideas	x	x	29

SPEAKING • Common Topics	IELTS	TOEFL	Page(s)
Travel and tourism (including online tourism)	x	x	111, 113, 115, 117, 119, 126
Cities and public spaces	x	x	95, 97, 100, 101, 103, 108
Fashion	x		21, 23, 27, 29, 36
Change	x	x	36, 39, 41, 51, 54
Stories and storytelling	x		3, 5, 9, 11, 15, 18
Advertising and advertisements	x		47, 48, 51, 52, 54
Humor	x		77, 81, 83, 90
Sports and teams	x		129, 130, 137
Health and hygiene	x	x	41, 47, 137
Animals	x		59, 62, 63
Emotions and experiences	x		136, 137
Sustainability	x		101, 108
Leaders and leadership	x	x	59, 65
Jobs	x	x	131
Data	x		135
The media	x	x	45

CREDITS

Illustrations: All illustrations are owned by © Cengage.